They Drink it in the Congo

Adam Brace was born in London in 1980. His first full-length play, *Stovepipe*, had an eight-week London run in collaboration with the National Theatre. It was shortlisted for the George Devine Award, named Best Political Theatre of the year by *Time Out*, nominated for a WhatsOnStage award and listed in the *Sunday Times* Best Twenty Theatre Events of the Decade. *They Drink it in the Congo* is his second full-length play. Shorter plays include *Midnight Your Time*, a one-woman show for Diana Quick. His first script for film, *Best*, won the 2013 Sundance London Short Film contest and was officially selected for Sundance Festival 2014 in Utah. Adam is Associate Dramaturg at Nuffield Theatre, Southampton, and is a regular director and script editor for live comedy.

also by Adam Brace from Faber

STOVEPIPE

ADAM BRACE

They Drink it in the Congo

FABER & FABER

First published in 2016
by Faber and Faber Limited
74–77 Great Russell Street
London WC1B 3DA

Typeset by Country Setting, Kingsdown, Kent CT14 8ES
Printed and bound by CPI Group (UK) Ltd, Croydon CR0 4YY

All persons, events and organisations in this play
are entirely fictitious.

A CIP record for this book
is available from the British Library

ISBN 978-0-571-33494-0

2 4 6 8 10 9 7 5 3 1

THIS PLAY IS DEDICATED TO

Mama Annie Matundu who hosted me in DRC,
found me contacts and guides, fed me and
laughed at my dancing

C & K who started my engagement with
their homeland and and who taught me so much

My agent Rosie Cobbe, who convinced me not
to give up on it. And even lent me her laptop
to finish it when both my computer and I were broke

Sebastian Born, who originally commissioned it, shaped
my thinking on it, helped me fund my trip to Congo and
even understood when local bribes didn't yield receipts

ACKNOWLEDGEMENTS

I talked to a lot of people while researching this play – my
thanking them does not mean they endorse the outcome.
My thanks to all the Congolese in London who have
talked to me over the past few years. A number of you
have specifically asked not to be named. Equally the NGO
professionals I have interviewed. I observed a number
of public meetings, campaigns, events and festivals on
Congo, but this play is not based on them or a reflection
on their success.

I began work on this play at the National Studio, thanks
to the brilliant support of Purni Morell. Rob Icke has
always believed in it and helped it find a home. Michael
Longhurst has pushed for the play to happen and helped
shape the final drafts.

Warmest thanks to Nounou Bootu and Victor Ilunga (both of whom have characters named after them who are *nothing* like them). Vava Tampa. Tamsin Larber. Mama Cecile for her hospitality. JJ Bola for hearing me out. Jean Christophe for looking after me in Congo. Stephen Carter. The English Department at University of Kinshasa. Dr David Garbin at UKC. Dr Zoë Marriage at SOAS. Professor George Nzongola Ntalaja. Dr Will Jackson and Dr Jo Sadgrove at Leeds University. Sophia Pickles. Anneke von Woudenburg and Human Rights Watch. Sue Lukes. Writing by Jason Stearns (*Dancing in the Glory of Monsters*), Dr Wa Gamoka Pambu, Professor George Nzongola Ntalaja, David Van Reybrouk, William Hothschild, Dr Zoë Marriage, Michaela Wrong, Anjam Sundaram, David Garbin (*Mediating the Sacred in the Congolese Diaspora*), In theatre terms: Dan Rebellato's *Theatre and Globalisation*. On folk tales: Angele Kadima-Nzuji Kabwasa (*Song of the Mermaid and Other Folk Tales from the Congo*), *Notes on the Folklore of the Fjort* by Richard Edward Dennett. Melvin Burgess's *Folk Stories from the Congo*.

My parents Nikki and Nigel Hopkins. Elaine Hopkins. Diane Brace. Cath and Mike and all at Moulin Ferrand. The brilliant Oliver Birch who helped develop the character of Tony. Vicky Jones, for her great input and for convincing me not to give up on it. John Ginman. Seb Armesto. Justin Audibert who directed and cast the first reading. Nick Payne. Charlotte Westenra. Chris Haydon. Sh!t Theatre. William Oldroyd. Chris Kelham. Ben and Tiff Woodsmith. Jimmy McGhie. NJHG Cartwright. Phoebe Waller-Bridge. Miriam Nabarro. Sergei Gratchev. Ella Hickson. Tobias Menzies. Rufus Norris for developing it and supporting it. Al Smith for being a diamond. Sam Hodges for being a great boss and friend. Becca Fuller, for brilliant ideas and for picking me off the floor. My brother Al for all the ritalin.

They Drink it in the Congo was first performed at the
Almeida Theatre, London, on 12 August 2016. The cast
was as follows:

Jenny / Intern / Meredith / Carmen Kirsty Besterman
Stef Fiona Button
Luis Richie Campbell
Maurice / Pastor Joshua Sidney Cole
William / Samo / Oliver / Kevin Tosin Cole
Huw / Hakan / Fred / Ian Roger Evans
Tony Richard Goulding
Kat / Alice / Patience / Suzanne Joan Iyiola
Anne-Marie Mweka Anna-Maria Nabirye
Nounou / Ira Coleman / Mama Beatrice Pamela Nomvete
Victor Richard Pepple
Oudry Sule Rimi

All other parts played by members of the company.

Musicians Joseph Roberts, Crispin Robinson, Alan Weekes

Direction Michael Longhurst
Design Jon Bausor
Composer and Music Direction Michael Henry
Lighting Jack Knowles
Sound Giles Thomas
Movement Direction Diane Alison-Mitchell
Casting Anna Cooper
Costume Supervision Sydney Florence
Dialect and Voice Coach Zabarjad Salam
Dialect Consultants and Translation
   Donovan Lee McGrath, Nickens Nkoso
Fight Direction Bret Yount

Characters

Oudry
a father from South Kivu, DRC, the voice
of digital technology. Congolese male, late thirties

Stephanie Cartwright
campaign co-ordinator.
White English female, about thirty

Anne-Marie Mweka
campaigner.
Congolese female, late thirties/forties

Tony Jarman
event consultant. White English male, about thirty

Luis
a leader in Les Combattants. Congolese male

Victor Malumbu
businessman. Congolese male, middle-aged

Huw Bennion
MP for Clwyd West. White Welsh male, forties

Kat
assistant to Stef, an intern.
Black British female, early twenties

Nounou
a neighbour of Anne-Marie.
Congolese female, late thirties/forties

Jenny Walton
Human Rights Monitor.
White English female, thirties/forties

Maurice
a Secretary in Les Combattants
Congolese male, forties/middle age

William
member of Les Combattants. Congolese male, twenties

Ira Coleman
author. African American female, forties/fifties

Suzanne
Anne-Marie's daughter.
Congolese British female, fourteen/fifteen

Oliver
a comedian. British Congolese male, twenties

Pastor Joshua
of New Jesus Church. Congolese male, middle-aged

Carmen Lankena
photographer. White American female, thirties

Samo Muwanga
Children of Conflict. Ugandan male, late twenties

Fred Fletcher
Conflict Mineral International.
White British male, forties

Alice Ekofo
DRC Horizon.
British Congolese female, early twenties

Patience
a village girl, Oudry's daughter.
Congolese female, twelve/thirteen

Mama Beatrice
her mother, Oudry's wife.
Congolese female, thirties

Meredith
a nurse. White Canadian female, twenties/thirties

Hakan
a kebab shop worker. White Turkish male

Ian Wandless
a podcaster. White British male

Militia Man
Congolese

Kevin
a policeman.
Black British male, late twenties/thirties

Intern
White British female

Diaspora 1
Congolese

Diaspora 2
Congolese

Journalist 1

Journalist 2

Poppy Eden Ellis
Ape Foundation.
An RP, late twenties, English voice

Radio
an American voice

THEY DRINK IT IN THE CONGO

Notes

☐ indicates an empty silence: a silence in which it's not clear what to say.

■ indicates a full silence: a silence in which things are actively not being said.

A forward slash (/) indicates the point at which the next character speaks over the remainder of the line.

No full stop at the end of a line means that the thought is unfinished, interrupted or part of a fluid exchange of dialogue.

Speech within angle brackets (< >) is in another language (Lingala, French, Swahili) and is spoken *without* Congolese accent – something comfortable for the speaker and the listener, approaching a 'neutral' English accent, manifesting ease of expression while offering ease of comprehension. Such speech can be surtitled in Lingala/ Swahili if it's felt this aids the clarity of the convention and the themes of the play.

Oudry is the voice of all the digital technology in the play. In a Congolese accent.

The play would benefit from a Congolese rumba band (or a smaller representation of one).

My stage directions are up for grabs, but give a strong indication of the *sort of thing*.

The action should be fluid and scenes/sections can flow into one another.

Part One

ONE
THE COMPASSION INDUSTRY

Anne-Marie, alone. She could be addressing us. Or an unseen character.

Anne-Marie Just another evening. Rich whites and Congolais. Dressed up smart to hear people talk about Congo. White words from black mouths. Maybe watch a rumba. And feel bad because of the problems. And feel good because we are caring. And everyone enjoys a little visit to Congo. But nobody has to go there.
 That's what this event is. And it has no value.

   Stef enters.

I'm sorry, Stephanie, but that's what this event will be.

Stef I will make sure it's not like that, Anne-Marie.

   Huw enters.

Huw What d'you think the main thing going against this festival is?

Stef Apart from money?

Huw Not money

Stef Apathy. Lack of Congolese support.

Huw The main thing against this festival. Is that it's pathetic.

Stef Right.
 Okay.

Huw Your festival's pathetic.

Stef Well, I.
Yeah. Well, I haven't organised it yet.

Anne-Marie No. Sorry. We Congolais, we have our own campaigns.

Stef Your protest yesterday. Did it appear in any British media?

Anne-Marie I cannot help what British media do.

Stef I think our festival can.

Huw It will be pathetic won't it? Most likely. A problem nobody understands, middle of the jungle, fucking miles away and it was never one of our colonies anyway. Waste of time.

Stef Sorry, why did you employ me to do it then?

Huw I just want you to argue your corner.

Stef I know, it's a very transparent tactic.

Anne-Marie No offence to you, Stephanie, but. No more white angels. Coming to help African fools. We help ourselves.

Stef But don't you protest because you want help?

Anne-Marie We want people to take hands from our pockets.

Tony enters.

Tony Take it you need my help.

Stef Tony! It's been too long! You smell good, what's that?

Tony Aftershave.

Stef I mean what brand

4

Tony Oh. One of the designer ones.

Stef Coffee?

Tony Love one.

Oudry Internal network:

Stef Can you send a coffee in, please, any available intern. Black, and a peppermint tea.

Tony That's very specific, black intern

Stef Tony

Tony That's when you know you've made it, you can specify the race of your intern

Stef Let's make these jokes when we're not in a government building.

Tony Hi, could I have an Amerindian bring me a plate of truffles please!

Stef Do you think you say these things ironically, Tony? Because the worry is you say them more. Ronically.

Huw The worry comes when you half believe that it *is* pathetic. Because the horror of Congo, and how difficult it is to make anyone care. Plus the time that you spent there. When that all weighs on you. This campaign *will* seem pathetic.

Anne-Marie So your campaign wants Congolese so it can seem authentic?

Stef No, Anne-Marie, the campaign wants to give Congolese a voice. It's even called 'CongoVoice'

Anne-Marie We have a voice, you don't *give* us a voice

Stef Yes, but can I be blunt. You don't know how to use it.

Anne-Marie And you don't know how to listen.

Tony What do I know about the place? Not much. I know a bit about their drinking habits.

Stef Is this a joke about UmBongo?

Tony Might be.

Huw But it is not pathetic. You're combining Congolese diaspora here with Western NGOs. Campaign backed by Parliament and a big festival to start with a bang. Something with the spirit and culture of Congo at its heart.

Oudry Telephone call

Stef I don't think that's me.

Suzanne enters with a phone outstretched.

Oudry Telephone call.

Suzanne It's Grandpapa again. He's talking crazy in Lingala

Anne-Marie I'm sorry my father's medication does this sometimes. (*On phone.*) <Papa no one is trying to kidnap you, he is from the hospital.> Suzanne, introduce yourself!

Suzanne (*no enthusiasm*) Pleased-to-meet-you.

Huw If it works you can raise awareness, lobby Parliament, lobby business. Change how we view Congo.

Tony They don't actually drink it there do they?

Stef What's the ratio of me mentioning Congo to people making a joke about UmBongo?

Tony Something like one to one?

Suzanne Another Congo thing, right?

Stef 'Fraid so.

Suzanne (*to Stef*) Gonna pay her?

Stef It doesn't really work like that.

Suzanne rolls her eyes.

Tony We're not actually a lobbying company we're a *PR* company.

Stef What events are you running for them?

Tony Currently it's a form of rights for women.

Anne-Marie (*to phone*) <I am just in a meeting in Westminster. Home soon.>

Tony The rights for women in certain industries to have more. Opportunities.

Stef Certain industries.

Tony Sort of. Performative arts.

Stef Oh God, it's strip clubs isn't it?

Tony Look, PR budgets are down, you can't always choose your clients. I fucking knew I shouldn't have come here.

Anne-Marie (*off phone*) We must finish.

Suzanne Can I have my phone please?

She takes it and starts leaving.

Stef Great meeting you, Suzanne.

Anne-Marie (*shakes*) English girl now. Doesn't speak Lingala.
    Stephanie, Congolese here try every day for back home.

Stef Let's channel that energy into making CongoVoice *truly* Congolese.

Anne-Marie (*laughs*) This event may be many things but truly Congolese is never one.

Stef How can I change that?

Anne-Marie You cannot.

Huw I cannot promise you'll still have a job in six months. If you *can* launch the festival, then there's a job running the campaign. And if you can't, you can always go back to – what was it?

Stef Freight insurance, no I can't

Huw Really?

Stef I walked out on them to do this. My references stink.

Huw So you're stuck in the Compassion Industry.

Tony What's the point?

Stef Raise awareness

Tony Of what?

Stef The problems of the Congo.

Tony Which are?

Stef How long have you got?

Tony I think the point is, it's about you.

Stef It's not.

Tony It's about you being born in Africa, in Kenya, and being guilty about it

Stef It's not. It's absolutely not. It maybe is a bit but it's mostly not.

Anne-Marie It's not because I don't trust. It's because if this event is white words from black mouths it has no value. And my community never will listen to me again.

Stef How about if I *guarantee* Congolese are present to vote on all campaign decisions?

Anne-Marie How many?

Stef How many would you want?

Anne-Marie One-third.

Stef How about
   No. One-third. Our committee will be one-third
Congolese. No Congolese, no festival. I promise. Will
you help?

Anne-Marie I will see you tomorrow at your meeting.

   She exits.

Huw Diaspora meeting tomorrow. Wear your best shit-
proof jacket.

Stef Could I quickly run some ideas / past you

Huw Sorry. No.

Stef No?

Huw Look: I'm not going to have time to be a sympathetic
ear. I'm not your boss, I'm the MP for Clwyd West. And
I've been in East Congo with you and I trust you. So
y'know, get on with it.

Tony I *can* use Google, you know. I do know why I'm
here. Your Congo campaign has no PR attached with a
press launch in a week. And you want me to do it for
very little money.

Stef Actually no money.

Huw Oh, one thing: the attack on the village. Distasteful
I know but.
   First-hand stuff. Really gets through to people.

   *Huw leaves. Tony and Stef are in her office. Portcullis
   House.*

Stef Tony I've missed you and this is as good a chance as
any to. Catch up.

Tony Simon no longer on the scene then?

Stef We split up when I went to SOAS.

Tony He always was against you doing a Master's.

Stef How d'you know that?

Tony You have a Kenya Airways sickbag on your wall. With handwriting on it.

Stef It's an aide mémoire.

> *Kat, a young black British intern, knocks and enters with drinks.*

Hey Kat.

■

Kat Anything else?

Stef Thanks, Kat.

> ■ *They watch Kat leave. Tony looks at Stef.*

Tony Wow. Can we get the Amerindian in, I do like truf—

> *Stef gestures 'enough', cutting him off.*

Stef We do have a press launch in a week. And I would love your expertise.

Oudry Suffering from nail fungus? You are not alone.

Stef Oh this bloody junk mail filter's playing up

Oudry Nearly one point eight million people in the UK suffer from nail fungus.

Stef Delete.

Oudry But there is an answer. Fungo-Clean / is a new powerful anti-nail fung—

Stef There's a meeting – Delete! Come tomorrow and I won't ask again

Tony Look, I will come to this meeting but

Stef Brilliant

Tony But please don't expect anything more

Stef I think you'll really see how much this means to people.

TWO
YOU FORGOT MANY THINGS ABOUT CONGO

Parliament. Meeting room.
  Most of the Congolese are dressed beautifully. People are both putting hands up to speak and speaking over each other.

Luis We have to *destroy* Congolese government!

Nounou No more destroy anything!

Victor There needs to be help to create the proper system.

Stef Sorry guys, one at a time please, we only have the room for an hour and a lot of people came twenty minutes late.

Maurice Parliament security takes fifteen minutes!

Luis Congo government is causing this!

Diaspora 2 You know old mothers were not raped until Ugandans and Angolans came in dere

Diaspora 1 You forgot many things about Congo

Anne-Marie Brothers sisters please! <We can't all speak at once>

Stef Can I just remind you again. This meeting is about your suggestions for a festival celebrating Congo – yes?

Diaspora 2 On the newspaper front today the Evening Standout one person stabbed

Oudry Telephone call

Diaspora 1 <No / Mum, that's the Amazon password, the Netflix password is my date of birth>

Diaspora 2 In Congo, one person stabbed every minute probably.

Victor <Sister, please. This is not helpful>

Stef No sorry, we *must* talk about the festival, we have very little time.

Diaspora 2 So you won't listen to me now!

Nounou Let her speak! You want us to keep order like a town meeting. But let us speak, it is from the heart! You look after children here, you forget ours!

   Applause.

Stef I understand that, Nounou, I really do. It's why I'm here.

Luis <She's here for her job>

Diaspora 2 <Exactly.> You are here for your job!

Nounou We are here so British government can hear us. Women raped every day, *hundreds* of women raped y'know

Stef I know, I do know / but what I need

Luis Not the only rape in Congo, British multinationals are rape our country everyday. British Virgin Islands the tax haven for our mineral wealth to fly from our hands.

Stef What I really need are suggestions / for the festival

Luis And you have this festival saying ya ya ya, it's so *terrible* in the Congo, here is a sad film, here is a bad picture of a boy, I wipe a tear

Stef Let's *celebrate* Congolese culture / for once.

Luis But don't stop mining my diamonds, my coltan for my cell phone, my laptop, don't stop mining my gold, don't stop mining because we are all rich from this. Isn't it?

Some applause, not Anne-Marie or Nounou.

Stef I hear that. I don't disagree with you. We are all linked by a deep concern for Congo. And I am proposing a positive way to channel that.

Victor We have this before, Miss Cartwright, with respect – people come to the Diaspora and interested to help, for three weeks, they say, 'We must do something.' And then – end of campaign, move jobs, they get bored. Now we help, uh, who uh, Angola! Now a flood in Pakistan. So why you're different?

Stef Because I'm not going away.

Maurice It's your job! If your job end you go away!

Stef It's more than a job.

Diaspora 2 <Is she an MP?>

Diaspora 1 <Just a secretary basically.>

Luis Excuse me, Miz Stephanie, I can't read your badge.

Stef Cartwright.

Luis Miz Cartwright, you are an MP?

Stef No, I'm not an MP.

Luis So you have no power?

Stef I'm co-ordinator of this festival but no elected power, no

Maurice Why should we listen to you then?

Stef Because *together* we can have some *power*.

Maurice <Oh good, we're in a Disney film.>

Stef (*pointed*) I'm sorry I don't understand you.

Luis What is your salary?

Stef We are getting British charities, Congolese charities / to work *together*

Luis What is your salary?

Maurice Yes. What salary?

Stef Mine, is that relevant?

Luis Yes.

Victor You can tell us, Miss Cartwright, how much they pay you?

Tony Fellas, there's a festival to organise, she doesn't have to answer / that

Stef It's fine, Tony

Luis How much?

Stef I'm paid about the average / wage I'd

Luis Say!

Stef Alright, if I worked a whole year – which I hope I do, cos it means we've been a success – then it'd work out about. Twenty-eight thousand pounds.

Luis Aha ha ha hah

Tony About a quarter of what she could be earning

Diaspora 1 A nice life for some eh

Tony It's really not much in London

Diaspora 2 We know how expensive London thank you, sir!

Tony She's a Cambridge graduate, seriously employable

Stef Tony!

Tony She's chosen to do this for *peanuts*

Luis More than many Congolais earn here

Nounou *Peanuts* he says

Diaspora 2 Yes, not me personally but many people earn less

Luis No, personally I earn more also but many don't

Maurice I am the same. <Of course I have my own business so>

Diaspora 1 My brother in Brussels is earning very well.

Maurice <But I'm thinking of many others>

Anne-Marie Eh, listen, this is great rudeness. <This woman's got the right to be paid, she works hard, I've got forty voicemails to prove it so – whatever you think of her she's at least trying>

Tony Can we stick to English?

Anne-Marie Respect please, it is fine to be angry, but don't give Congolais a bad name

Luis She is paid and she doesn't know anything about Congo.

Oudry Telephone call

Stef I don't claim to know everything about your country but I'm not ignorant either. I've read every book I can find

Maurice <Ah, European books about Congo!>

Oudry Telephone call

Stef Can we have all phones off, please!
  Look I do know this is weird. I'm not from there. What can I tell you about your country? All I can tell you is that I mean what I'm doing.
  I was in South Kivu six months ago visiting the International Medical Corps. There was a rape attack on a village. We were the first outsiders to the site of the attacks. They took me as an emergency pair of hands. I met a man who had been forced to sexually assault his own daughter. He had a hole in his head. It was the strangest colour almost like a tropical fruit. Five minutes left – I've found some rumba bands who are now based in Belgium

Luis The only people who are really doing anything in London are the Combattants de Londres.

Anne-Marie <Oh here we go>

Stef A Congo festival's got to have a rumba band, hasn't it?

Luis And this group of men, the Combattants de Londres.

Maurice They stand up and say the truth

Anne-Marie <You are *in* the group the Combattants>

Luis They are working for a free Congo.

Anne-Marie <You walk around like a soldier when there is no war here>

Maurice <Ah the coconut. White on the inside!>

Nounou <Eh, you shut up, brother>

Anne-Marie <These Combattants must really give the President insomnia>

Luis <Find a white husband yet?>

Anne-Marie <Pathetic>

Tony English please.

Victor <Brothers, enough>

Anne-Marie These men are all Mobutist

Luis No no you listen

Anne-Marie His father had a job in the past government. Now his family has no power

Luis This woman is not the normal Congolais, she has lost her culture

Maurice She wants to be European.

Anne-Marie Power is all they care for, not their country, not the people

Maurice Stop your nonsense of lies

Anne-Marie Sad men

Luis I refuse to be abuse and lied about. This festival is not for Congolese!

Luis and Maurice exit, voices erupts, the meeting is finishing.

Stef Well, thanks, everyone. You'll be hearing more this week!

People leave.
Nounou and Stef, Victor and Anne-Marie remain.

Victor <Sister Anne-Marie – well said today.>

Anne-Marie <They're *your* friends.>

Victor <They're my neighbours.
I heard your organisation is funding a woman's refuge in Goma. My organisation sent digital imaging to a hospital in Goma last year.>

Anne-Marie <Very good. When did you last go back to visit your mama?>

Victor <I, uh. Soon. I'll go back soon.>

Anne-Marie leaves.

Nounou One man who does much for Congo – have you talked with Pastor Joshua?

Stef Pastor Joshua. From New Jesus in Tottenham?

Nounou He is a good way for bringing the Congolais.

He leaves. Stef and Victor remain.

Victor Would you be interested in a Congolese poet?

Stef A Congolese poet? Absolutely

Victor Who writes in English?

Stef That's exactly the sort of thing

Victor I know one. But it is quite, in secret.

Stef That's great, Victor. Thank you.

THREE
GOD IS TECHNOLOGY

New Jesus Church in Tottenham Hale.
  Pastor Joshua addresses his loud congregation.

Pastor Joshua God is technology!

When a revelation is coming it is like a cell phone, driiing driiing, in your heart. A good relationship with God, the frequency is ve-ry good, the signal is ve-ry strong. You are living a bad life, in conflict with people, your reception will be bad. I say for you to get connected because technology is holy!

Stef is outside reading her tablet.

Oudry Get Connected! With New Jesus Church, Tottenham Hale!

Pastor Joshua Please, brothers and sisters, no prayers of anger against individuals. No malice.

Oudry Find Pastor Joshua on LinkedIn.

Pastor Joshua The Lord commands us not to curse but to bless him to be vengeful on our behalf.

Oudry New Jesus Website Question of the Day:

Pastor Joshua And God wills us to send money as well as prayers.

Oudry How different would your finances look if Jesus was your accountant?

Pastor Joshua On the church website you can donate through direct debit, Moneygram or Western Union to help our mission in Kivu.

A room in the church. Stef and Pastor Joshua alone.

Pastor Joshua I know Anne-Marie, her Papa Albert comes to church, but he is ill today. Yes, I worry she is a lost woman.

Stef Lost?

Pastor Joshua She stirs the trouble. And she has no God.

Stef Pastor the reason I've come to you. Is our festival cannot function without Congolese community leaders.

Pastor Joshua But of course, you will not have the same ideas as we.

Stef If our committee isn't at least one-third Congolese, the festival doesn't go ahead.

Pastor Joshua Really it is the churches in the diaspora who can help. New Jesus has a mission in Kivu, a school. We send medical equipments.

Stef Yes. you do a lot, it's why I got in contact.

Pastor Joshua Excuse me, I am going to have a yoghurt.

Stef Okay

Pastor Joshua After service I like a pro-biotic yoghurt. Would you care for one?

Stef Oh. Uh
   No.

Pastor Joshua It's a drinking yoghurt, not the uh, y'know, spoon / yoghurt

Stef No, thank you, but that's kind

Pastor Joshua Do you know how the bacteria in a pro-biotic yoghurt works?

Stef I don't.

Pastor Joshua Well.
   I don't either.

Stef Ha, okay, I thought for a moment you were going to say y'know, 'Well it's like the problems of the Congo,' ha

Pastor Joshua No, why would I say that?

Stef I know, you wouldn't.

Pastor Joshua It's got nothing to do with Congo. It's just a yoghurt.

Stef No, I know.
Pastor, your support would be so important for us.

Pastor Joshua You have my support.

Stef Really?

Pastor Joshua Ye-s, very much so.

Stef Brilliant. We have a press launch in three days, but more important at this stage would be to have you at a committee meeting.

Pastor Joshua I really don't have time for meetings

Stef Well, we'll say you have given us your blessing?

Pastor Joshua I have not blessed anything.

Stef Not actual blessing but.
We can tell other Congolese in London that you

Pastor Joshua Ah no.

Stef Sorry?

Pastor Joshua I do give you my support. I will pray for you.

Stef So we can say you support us?

Pastor Joshua Mm? No. Not my name on anything

Stef Why not?

Pastor Joshua You have my prayers.

Stef You support us but we can't tell anyone?

Pastor Joshua My name and my image really belong to the church.

Stef Pastor, there is a horrific wound in your home country. And I am trying to get people, British people to look at it. Because once they've looked at it they won't be able to pretend it's not there. Can you at least put your name to that?

■

Pastor Joshua Y'know. You have this festival about Congo.
But all you can really find out about.
Is yourself.
Or your own country.

FOUR
HE WILL DIED HERE

Stef's office. Tony and Kat.

Tony You'll be too young but. It was a tropical fruit drink basically. And there was this advert with a monkey and, I think a marmoset.
And they sang / 'UmBongo UmBongo'

Kat Yeah, I looked it up but why does everyone ask about it?

Tony People don't know much else about the place.

Kat After the stuff I had to read today, I'd rather I didn't know anything about the place.

Tony Did you not *ask* to work on this then?

Kat Sustainable waste solutions you need a Master's.

Tony What's this sickbag she's had framed?

Kat Oh, she wrote it on the flight out of Congo. She didn't want to write on her phone because of. Y'know. So she has it there to sort of. Remind her how she felt.

Tony Can I read it?

Stef enters.

Stef Hello, sorry to keep you.

Kat Huw Bennion wants to speak with you about that message / from Les

Stef Thank you, Kat, we don't need to talk about that now.

Kat is a little put out. She leaves.

Tony I enjoyed the meeting. Imagine if you told them what you really earned

Stef I did.

Tony Jesus, lucky your dad left you the flat, eh?

Stef When did I tell you that?

Tony Just. Presumed.

Stef My dad would be proud of this, he loved Africa.

Tony Didn't he want to be buried there? Buried in Kenya on your old land?

Stef Yes well. He did but. The people who own it now said we couldn't.

Tony Where is he buried?

Stef He's buried in Surbiton.
    Now. Victor, who was there yesterday – lovely guy – knows a Congolese poet who writes in English. That's a start, right?

Tony Sure

Stef We can't announce any acts at the press launch. But the story is:

Festival of Congolese culture. Kicks off a campaign backed by Parliament. Congolese here will help run it. Finish with loose informative Q'n'A about the crisis / and the festival.

Tony Stephanie.
I said I'd come to the meeting.

Stef begins tapping on her smartphone.

And it's obviously very. Horrific. And I do have every sympathy. But.
Sorry. No.

Stef ■

Tony I did tell you.

Stef ■
You did. Thank you.

Oudry Messenger:

Stef It's been great to see you again. I understand.

Oudry Kat, could you come in please

Tony Good luck, y'know, it's just not for me

Stef No.

Tony So y'know. Sorry. Not to say that you and I can't

Oudry Look worried and tell me I should read that email.

Stef Where's my kiss?

She kisses him on the cheek and gives him a long hug.

Tony Right.

Stef Back to the day job then.

Tony Yup

Stef Helping those poor girls express themselves.

Tony Well, I'll see you.

Kat enters.

Kat Sorry to interrupt I think you should read your email.

Stef Really?

Kat Uh. Yes?

Stef Sorry Tony, hold one sec

Tony I'll go, I was going anyway

Stef No no, wait. You need to see this.

Tony reads. Kat exits.

Oudry 'From Les Combattants de Londres. We Congolese residents in London stroke UK are warning you to cancel this events for your safety. We can promise those involved will be kill. Tell all Congolese making trips to London for this festival, if he try he will died here. Also true for sponsor Evian Water. We cannot allow such events by the responsible for the Silent Genocide in our country. Best regards, for Congolese resistance. Les Combattants de Londres. We are watching the following Congolese: Anne-Marie Mweka'

Tony That's Anne-Marie who spoke up at the meeting?

Oudry 'And all others Congolais who collaborate. 'Also the English accomplices: Huw Bennion MP'

Tony He'll take 'English' worse than a death threat.

Stef Keep going

Tony Oh fuck, you've got a death threat

Oudry Stephanie Cartwright

Stef Read on.

Oudry Also:

Tony Oh fuck I've got a death threat

Oudry Tony Jarman

Tony I only turned up to watch

Stef I know

Tony I'm not even involved

Stef I know

Tony How the hell did they get my name?

Stef You were wearing a badge

Tony Fuck's sake.

☐

But it's typical empty crap right, intimidation from impotent people

Stef Yeah, I mean well, no. They recently assaulted a kid from LSE and set his car on fire.

Tony Why?

Stef His dad edits a government-friendly newspaper

Tony Right, so. Police then?

Stef Absolutely.

☐

Tony This is shit.

Stef Yeah.

Tony This is shit for you, Stef, I'm sorry.

Stef Well. Hardest for you in a way

■

Tony How's that?

Stef Because I suppose. No.

Tony What?

Stef No, don't worry

Tony Go on, what?

Stef I suppose the worry is it looks like you're running scared.

□

Tony I don't see how.

Stef It might look a bit – Tony was on the project, there's been a death threat, Tony's not on the project.

Tony Well it's

Stef Yeah

Tony It's not an issue, is it?

Stef No sure. Not for me but

Tony Yes?

Stef ■

Tony ■
I'm saying it's not an issue.

Stef Is it not?

Tony No.

Stef How come?

Tony Cos I am buggered if I'm going to be intimidated

Stef Seriously?

Tony Yep.

Stef You mean

Tony Really, I'm buggered if I'll let a death threat scare me off. Death threats? For just organising a festival

Stef It's ridiculous.

Tony These people need to understand this isn't Congo, this is London.

Stef Pretty sure they do understand that. But *thank you*. You're really gonna help me out?

Tony Yeah, I mean. Yes. The press launch at least. Send me all the copy and a list of journos – I'll make some calls. And we should live-stream the launch online. No one'll watch it of course but we will seem modern and accessible.

Stef Thank you, Tony.
  Come to steering committee tomorrow, will you, we need to get a vote through. We're going to guarantee one-third of our committee are Congolese.

Tony Nothing's ever fucking simple with you, is it.

  He exits.   Stef starts tapping into her tablet.

Oudry Messenger: Kat, thank you, you're owed one large tub pralines and cream, love Stef.

FIVE
GOLD IN OUR THROATS

Maurice's internet café, Turnpike Lane. William is watching football online.

William <It cuts out.>

Maurice <Eh, when Papa Luis is here>

William <It keeps cutting out.>

Maurice <William, when Papa Luis is here, don't say anything to anger him.>

William <Luis likes me. He likes men of action. This game keeps cutting out.>

Maurice <Yeah, it cuts out>

William <Can you fix it?>

Maurice <You don't know you're born.>

William <Meaning?>

Maurice <Meaning, you're watching an illegal live feed of premiership football, you accept it sometimes cuts out. Like I accepted that the car radio of my cousin, with twenty of us crowded round it, listening to Arsenal in ninety-four.
Would cut out.
Except you're fucking watching it aren't you. For free.>

William <Bergkamp.>

Maurice <What about him?>

William <You had Bergkamp in ninety-four.>

Maurice <No, we had Bergkamp in ninety-five ninety-six, I left Congo ninety-five, that's the year we got Bergkamp.>

■

William If we're talking about English football can we talk in English?

Maurice I talk in English all day. <Allow me the pleasure of talking in Lingala>

■

William <You know I think you're really in trouble.>

Maurice <Do you?>

William <A man who is basically mad with his own pride. In life you need to change. As a human being it's not good to resist change. And Arsène Wenger needs to change.>

Maurice <He built something beautiful.>

William <Like a Kardashian, beautiful but useless>

Maurice <There are higher things in the world than just winning, Arsenal are not just a machine for turning games into wins>

William <They've made that very obvious>

Maurice <They are an expression of humanity.>

William <Arsenal fans really will say anything.>

Maurice <Did you see the email?>

William <No, brother, I didn't get a chance this week, they're very long.>

Maurice <The email sent to Parliament. The festival email.>

William <Ah. The threat. Yeah. I liked it.>

Maurice <Luis sent it before I looked. It's badly written.>

William <If you wrote it, it'd be five pages long, brother.>

Maurice <The English was terrible.> 'Those involve will be kill'.
    <Mixing tenses.> 'He will died here.'
    <How are they gonna take us seriously with emails like that?>

William <They take us seriously when we back our threats, Papa Maurice.>

Maurice <When we have attention, we don't need threats.>

William <Threats is like. This is more important than what you think. We will do anything for this. All you people. Talking. Making money. You won't do anything. But *we*. We will do anything.>

Maurice <Maybe you will.
Stay here. I have a package for Luis.>

Maurice exits. William watches football. It cuts out again, he's frustrated.

Hakan enters, a white Turkish man.

William Sorry, man. Can you wait, he is one minute.

Hakan places fifty pence on the counter.

Hakan Just the toilet.

He disappears into the shop. Maurice returns.

Maurice <Is this your money?>

William <Uh no, this guy came in and put that there.>

Maurice <Which guy? Not a Turkish guy?>

William <Maybe.>

Maurice Hey, no more shitting in my café! You hear me! Get out here, Hakan!

William <What's happening?>

Maurice No shits I told you.
    <This guy comes here and shits like four times a week.>
No shits man!
    <It's too late, he's shitting in there. This guy works in Okabasi and they have a toilet that's both staff and customers, so he started coming and laying these spicy shits here.

I mean just imagine what the guy eats in that kebab shop.

And I said, 'Toilets are for customers only,' so now he comes here and pays fifty p to block my toilet.>

Eh, stop this, Turkish, we are not a public shit house! <Really gets me angry.>

Luis enters.

William <Ah Papa Luis!>

Luis <Y'know, brothers, there are pleasures that life provides when a poor man feels like he is rich.>

Maurice <Welcome, Papa Luis!>

Luis <Even when I feared I would die every day, insects taking my country hostage, even then – I would sit down with a man next to me, and maybe he saved me maybe I'd saved him, maybe I never saw him before, and my arm was still locked like this, like the rifle's still there, and maybe his arm was locked so too, but we'd have a bottle of Primus, and it was like gold in our throats. We were rich. This week, brothers, I started to feel rich again. I have the prize.>

William <Prize, Papa Luis?>

Luis <Go to the boot of my car, William. Bring in the biggest thing you find.>

William leaves.

Maurice <You know, I'd really prefer it if you let me write the emails.>

Luis <Did our package arrive?>

Maurice <Came today.>

He produces a package. Luis takes it and pulls out a revolver.
Maurice is shocked.

Hakan comes out of the toilet and Luis stuffs the revolver away.

Maurice That is the last time, my friend. Five pounds next time!

Hakan See you tomorrow, man.

He waves him away and leaves.

Maurice <Brother, this is not the way.>

■

William enters with a framed picture of the President of DR Congo.

William <Eh, this is some picture.>

Luis <Because it's from the consul.>

William <No way!>

Maurice <Very symbolic.>

William <The London Embassy?>

Luis <The London Embassy of DRC.>

William <Brilliant.>

Luis <He will see it and know it's off the wall of his own Embassy in London.>

William <How d'you get it?>

Luis <It says nothing here is safe. It says fuck you Kabila, we can mobilise, we can infiltrate your building, we can take your image and show our boot to it.>

William <How did you get in the Embassy to steal this?>

Luis <It's not important how>

Maurice <Well>

Luis <Is it?>

Maurice <It was in a skip at the back cos they had a new one done.>

William <Ha! So really we're just doing their recycling for them.>

Luis calmly puts a hand to William's throat.

<Papa Luis, relax. I'm sorry, it's a joke – take it easy.>

Luis <'Take it easy'. You like computers, William. On my desktop, I have an image from Google Earth. It's my road in Kin. My family house. I know the man who lives in our house now. A military judge called Philippe. Twelve rooms he has there. Two together are bigger than my whole flat in East Ham. I live in a pocket. He lives in a whole suit. His wife sleeping where my mother should sleep. His feet walking on stairs my father built. His children playing in our garden – our garden, where we grew everything: cassava, kisantu, pawpaw, dioamond, mangoes. Unforgettable fucking mangoes. What they think are mangoes here in Morrisons or Tesco, that is yellow cardboard soaked in water. If you haven't tasted one of my mango, you haven't had a real fucking mango. This has come from the soil that has a richness you can't buy. And you know what he does with that soil?
Judge Phillipe?
He parks his fucking car on it.
And he has a shit Japanese car.
My father had the fucking pride in himself to drive around in a French car. That garden is mud and dirt and

34

shit and everything's dying or died. So, brother William, I don't take it easy. I do find it hard to relax. But when we're all back in Kin, I'll force my way through Judge Philippe's door, put my hand over his wife's mouth and throw his children in the gutter. Then I'll hold him by his hair and open his belly with a kitchen knife. So that everything spills out. The rich food he ate in our kitchen. The shit he swallowed in court. And all the spunk he sucked from the President's diseased cock. All foaming in pools around our feet.

And then, maybe, I'll take it easy.

We have traitors all around us. Here in London as much as home. This traitor festival, these people from Parliament, rewriting the righteous story of our home. So I don't take it easy and neither should you.

But for now, we have this prize. This picture. Next week we make a film with this prize, a movie, a YouTube. That they can see here and back home.>

☐

Maurice <It's just. The camera's broken.>

William <Nokia Lumia Twelve Megapixel, who needs a camera?>

Luis <So next week you shoot the film.>

William <Like, direct it!>

Maurice <Next week everyone's away. We won't have the numbers.>

Luis <The Combattants are strong we have to keep momentum. We make the film next week.>

William <Is our movie gonna mention the festival?>

Luis <There is no need to mention a thing that does not exist.>

35

Maurice <It may be about to, brother. They announced their press launch.>

Luis <Indeed. Then we must mobilise more than our mouths, and next week's video will be a / call to arms.>

Maurice <Next week will be too late, brother. The launch is in two days.>

Luis <How was I not made aware of this?>

Maurice <It was in my email.>

Luis ■
<My paps used to say 'Luis! Throw a dead fish in the Congo river as hard as you like. It will not swim.'
So what do we do William?>

■

William <Is the fish the festival?>

Luis <Yeah that's how I was thinking about it.>

■

William <Make sure the fish is dead before it hits the water?>

Luis (*to Maurice*) <He'll go far.>

SIX

VIRTUE SIGNALLING

A meeting room in Portcullis House. Stef, Tony, Anne-Marie, Victor, Nounou and Fred. The meeting has not started, people are talking among themselves.
Jenny enters.

Jenny Not late, am I?

Stef No. Jenny, bang on time.

Jenny I never said congratulations on being made Festival Co-ordinator.

Stef Thank you. I think ultimately Huw wanted to go with someone they already knew.

Jenny Yes, I think that's exactly what it was.

Samo enters. The meeting begins.

Stef Good morning, everyone. Welcome to this incredibly exciting first steering committee meeting for CongoVoice. The people in this room now will make the major decisions for this campaign. And today we have an important vote to ensure Congolese voices are at the heart of CongoVoice.

But look, let's cut to chase – we need to address the death threats that we received during the week.

I'm aware they may have affected numbers today.

But may I say: I think that backing down because of a cowardly threat would be sending the wrong message. I'd particularly like to applaud the bravery of the Congolese women coming here today in full knowledge –

Nounou puts her hand up.

– of that threat and in defiance of it. Yes, Nounou?

Nounou There's been a death threat?

Stef Yes.

Nounou From Les Combattants?

Stef It was signed Les Combattants, yes.

Nounou gets up and gathers her things.

Nounou Sorry.

She leaves.

Anne-Marie Her kids are at school with their kids.

Stef Right. That brings me to the next thing, attendance – if those of you intending on staying could go round quickly stating names and the organisation you're representing.

Jenny Jenny Walton, Human Rights Monitor. Also Jeremy McGuire from Streetchild asked me to send his apologies.

Anne-Marie Anne-Marie Mweka, CWPJ, Congolese Women for Peace and Justice.

Fred Fred Fletcher, Conflict Mineral International.

Victor Victor Malumbu, HopCon, Hope for Congo.

Samo Samo Muwanga, Children of Conflict.

Tony And I'm Tony Jarman, no charity, but I'm event consultant, and can I just say at this point that as someone who is under a death threat myself, I'd like to

Stef Alright, thanks, Tony

Tony I'm doing PR basically.

Stef And I'm Stephanie Cartwright, co-ordinator of this festival.

Oudry Skype for Business – conference request.

Stef We are also being joined by Poppy Eden Ellis of the Ape Foundation on conference call. Hello, Poppy!

Poppy (*voice-over*) Hi, everyone

All Hello!

Poppy (*voice-over*) Sorry I can't be there.

Stef You somewhere exotic, Poppy?

Poppy (*voice-over*) No I'm in Crouch End my childcare fell through.

Stef Well. We're trying to make our meetings as paperless as possible so please all follow on your screens.

Oudry Vote: CongoVoice festival must have at least a one-third Congolese presence on the steering committee.

Jenny I do feel the make-up of the committee hardly needs legislating.

Anne-Marie This is one way to help Congolais trust you.

Jenny Sure, but with respect, many Congolese who said they'd come today haven't shown.

Victor There *have* been threats.

Jenny Do we want inappropriate people simply because they're Congolese?
    And I know what I sound like. Elitist. Culturally insensitive. But I've had this with the Iranian diaspora, the Zimbabweans, even the Burmese

Victor Madam, not all diaspora are the same.

Stef We can't have a Congolese festival that excludes the voices of the Congolese, especially when we call it CongoVoice.

Anne-Marie (*chuckling*) That would be *really* stupid.

Jenny *We* didn't call it that.

Stef No alright, I did. Let's vote on it.
    One-third Congolese on the Steering Committee? In favour.

A majority of hands go up. Stef scans them.

Poppy (*voice-over*) I'm putting my hand up, by the way.

Stef That's passed. It's not a drastic thing, if we continue as we are we're fine: nine people, we have three Congolese, that's a third.

Anne-Marie No. Samo is not Congolese.

Stef Oh. God, I'm so sorry.

Samo I am from Uganda, but we of course have interest in the issue of child soldiers.

Stef Of course, sorry, I shouldn't have presumed.

Samo It's fine. I can't tell always Welsh and whatnot.

Stef No, but. I should've known.
  We don't quite have one-third Congolese. But by next meeting, that will change.

Jenny I hope your confidence is well placed, Stephanie, I really do.

Stef Thanks, Jenny, I'm sure we all value that positivity.
  A word about the press launch. Anne-Marie and I will present. I know that a lot of you can't be there but it *is* being live-streamed so please tweet about it and retweet us we are already at 1,100 followers which is a *start* / but we can

Tony Tell them about Harry

Stef (*shoots Tony a look*) Well, I don't want to make too much of it, but one of our followers is the British Oscar winner Harry Jandrell, who Tony and I were at university with.

Jenny One celebrity follower does not a campaign make.

Stef And as you'll see I'm not suggesting it does.

Oudry Social Media Policy: Moving Beyond Virtue Signalling.

Jenny So we're *beyond* getting likes and follows are we?

Stef No, but we want to convert them into active engagement. People in rooms, making positive investments. Not just retweeting us to signal their virtue to others.

Jenny And are you seriously suggesting we don't use viral content?

Stef I'm suggesting videos instantly shared and instantly forgotten don't work. Kony2012

Oudry Core Campaign Themes.

Stef The campaign will make consistent advocacy messages.

Fred Yep.

Stef Obviously for some this is second nature – are we happy with our themes? A?

Oudry Women: victims of war. Rape as a weapon. Representation.

Anne-Marie Absolutely.

Stef Great, B?

Oudry Children: child soldiers. Mortality rate.

Samo Very good.

Stef Finally C?

Oudry Natural resources.

Stef So they're the core themes, what I'd like / to do *now*

Poppy (*voice-over*) Just to clarify, do natural resources include gorillas?

    ☐ *Glances exchanged.*

Jenny They don't.

Stef I s'pose strictly speaking they could?

Fred We-ell, not really.

Poppy (*voice-over*) Why not?

Fred In Congo the natural resources we're talking about are gold, diamonds, coltan, cassiterite, tin, uh tungsten. Mined at great human cost and used by multinationals to make the world's technology.

Poppy (*voice-over*) I agree it's terrible, but I haven't heard anything about gorillas.

Jenny I think it could be confusing, conflict minerals, and then gorillas tacked on the end.

Fred Yeah, I don't think it / helps us

Poppy (*voice-over*) That kind of makes me wonder why I'm here.

☐

Tony Flakey babysitter, wasn't it?

Poppy (*voice-over*) We want assurance *today* that part of the advocacy agenda, probably natural resources, must be ape-related.

Fred That'd be diluting our message on conflict minerals and we'd walk.

Anne-Marie You love apes so much, where is your love for the naked ape?

Stef We will try to accommodate everyone.

Poppy (*voice-over*) Well, I think the festival is trying to secure our funding without granting proportional advocacy points and I'm afraid we'd walk too.

Stef Well *I'm* afraid that in light of five million dead and mass rapes every week, we might not be able to *lead* on gorillas in the mist.

Poppy (*voice-over*) Whose voice was that? Was that the co-ordinator?!

Jenny I'm afraid it was.

Fred More a case of 'Gorillas will be missed'.

Tony Very strong, Fred.

Poppy (*voice-over*) Look, I'm under strict instructions. I can't spend our 20K like this. Good luck, guys.

Oudry Signing off.

Fred We meeting next week then or should I not hold my breath?

Jenny We don't currently have a functioning committee, we don't have one-third Congolese and we've just lost twenty thousand pounds.

Stef We will have the numbers we need. And the finances.
    Don't delete it from your diaries. Let's move on.

HOW LONG HAVE YOU GOT?

Outside. Morning. Stef is tapping on her tablet.

Oudry CongoVoice Twitter: watch our campaign launch this morning on Periscope live from Westminster. We want your questions for the Q'n'A!
    Tweet.

She swipes and begins reading. She could be walking? Or waiting?

Crazy Celebrity Sideboob: Red Carpet Special.

She swipes again.

Editorial: luxury technology is enhancing our lives.
    It is changing our conception of who we are.

Stef is being watched.

Phones and tablets are sold to us as having souls. Like the power figures Nkishi – objects inhabited by fetish spirits in the Congo basin – they appear to contain life. Not simply objects made with human energy. From lifeless matter sourced with exploited labour.

But as something that has human energy itself.

A man in a mask walks straight up to Stef and throws a waterbomb at her.

She screams. The man runs. Maybe pedestrians react in confusion?

Stef is left covered in a red liquid. Her skin is stained red. She is helped away.

A conference room. Tony is directing Kat on a raised platform.

Tony Okay now, let's hear Stef's mic. Now Anne-Marie's. Bit less gain on that. Nice.

Anne-Marie enters.

Anne-Marie Scarf? Or no scarf?

Tony For the launch probably no scarf, but it is a very nice scarf.

You look absolutely right. Elegant, distinguished.

Kat, can you check if Stef's come through reception. She's not answering.

Kat leaves. ■

Y'know nerves are actually our body's way of providing us with focus.

Anne-Marie I'm not nervous.

Tony So Stephanie tells me you're a scientist

Anne-Marie I am trying to finish a PhD, if that makes me a scientist.

Tony What's your field?

Anne-Marie It's a very small field.

Tony But the small field is in a bigger field, right?

Anne-Marie Always.

Tony So what's the bigger field?

Anne-Marie Pain.

Tony Pain? Pain *is* a big field. What sort of pain do you look at? Back pain? Front pain? Thomas Paine?

Anne-Marie (*dry*) Well, I can see you have a science background.

Tony Hey, do you know the best sort of pain to look at?

Anne-Marie I would say, the pain of the rich.

Tony Ha. That's very good.
  That's actually better than what I was gonna say.

Anne-Marie What were you going to say?

Tony No, don't worry, it's definitely better.

Anne-Marie (*laughs*) Well I don't study rich pain sadly, I am investigating neural correlates of interindividual differences in the subjective experience of pain.

Tony Bit of an obvious choice. Got long left?

Anne-Marie I have a daughter, I care for my father so

Tony So might take a while then?

Anne-Marie Sadly, I think so

Tony Sounds *pain*ful.

Anne-Marie laughs.

You actually laugh at my jokes.

Anne-Marie Yes, I was laughing because *you* thought it was funny.

Stef enters hurriedly, a scarf wrapped around her face.

Stef Guys. Don't freak out.

Stef removes the scarf.

Tony Fuck, are you alright

Anne-Marie Eh

Stef I've been sprayed with red ink or something, it's okay, don't freak out

Kat enters and sees Stef.

Kat Ohmygod, are you alright?

Anne-Marie Are you in pain?

Kat D'you need an ambulance?

Tony Who did it!

Stef No, but it seems like it's stained me.

Tony Who did it?

Stef A man.

Tony A black man?

Kat and Anne-Marie can't help looking at him.

Well, it's a fair question.

Stef I don't know, his face was hidden.

Kat Have you called the police?

Anne-Marie Wait. I know this.

Anne-Marie sniffs the liquid.

Yes, it's Eosin.

Stef What's that?

Anne-Marie It's disinfectant, the Belgians use. On wounded children.
This was Les Combattants.
But you will be fine, it will make a stain for a few days.

Stef A few *days*.

Tony Fuckers

Stef First I thought it was acid, then I thought maybe fake blood.
Then I didn't know what to think

Kat Did you call the police?

Stef I came straight here, because of the launch.

Tony Forget about the press launch!

Stef No, I can do it.

Anne-Marie Of course we must cancel.

Stef We can't.

Tony We *can*.

Stef We'll lose the press. It's hard enough getting them here once, to then say not today someone's got red shit on their face

Anne-Marie Eosin.

Stef If we postpone, we won't get exposure, we're finished.

Anne-Marie No, Stephanie.

Stef After the first minute everyone will get used to it.

They look at her sceptically.

Well I *am* doing it and you're all gonna have to lump it.

Tony Stef, if it's being filmed, periscoped and photographed – the story will change from the campaign to 'Charity woman attacked with red *whatever*'

Anne-Marie Eosin.

Tony The story belongs to the fuckers who did it. And it might even scare more people off.

Stef ■
My God, I hate it when you're right.

Anne-Marie I do it alone.

Stef Anne-Marie. We can't.

Anne-Marie It's called CongoVoice. I am Congolese, I have a voice.

Stef This event is for a British audience. We need to present it as a partnership. Congolese diaspora *and* British NGOs with Parliament

Tony What about Huw Bennion?

Stef He's in Wales.

Tony What does the person actually need to do?

Kat (*to Stef*) Just chair the event, introduce the campaign, right?

Stef We've got African, British African journalists out there. I'd suggest you, Tony, if you didn't know absolutely fuck all about Congo.

Tony I know what they don't drink.
Look I should do this. How much do I really need to know?

Stef The history of the problems of the Congo.

Tony Right. All of them?

Stef Unless you want to insult people with your ignorance and ruin our campaign.

Tony But that's the only obstacle to me doing it?

Stef Well, I mean. Probably, but it's a pretty serious / obstacle

Anne-Marie One of the steering committee? Jenny?

They all look to Stef. ∎

Stef Jenny Walton, who wants my job?

Anne-Marie She has experience. Always near Westminster.

Stef We could we could call her but, I mean, it might confuse the press about who was co-ordinating the whole –

She gets her smartphone out.

Of course. Of course we should call her.

Oudry Calling: Jenny Human Rights Monitor.

Tony Y'know what, I'm good at stuff like this

Oudry Answerphone.

Stef Jenny, it's Stephanie Cartwright, if you're anywhere near the press launch do urgently come and find us.

Anne-Marie Okay, and what about Kat?

They all look at Kat. Kat almost physically hides.

Kat I can't speak in front of people.

Tony I'll do it – I'm actually better under pressure than Stef

Stef Bullshit

Tony Like when I did that bungee jump.

Anne-Marie You don't know Congo.

Stef *You* did a bungee jump?

Tony You watched me

Stef No

Tony For *your* college charity.

Stef I can't imagine *you* doing a bungee jump

Tony You don't have to imagine it because you watched me.

Anne-Marie Who is my partner for this launch?

Tony How long have we got?

Stef Ten minutes.

Kat We need to give them five to set up.

Tony So, fire away then. Whenever I ask about the problems of Congo everyone says, 'How long have you got?' Well, I've got five minutes.

Kat Four and a half

Tony I work with lobbyists, I pick up stuff quickly. Just tell me the problems of Congo in four and half minutes.

Stef and Anne-Marie look at each other. Anne-Marie is unhappy but relents.

Stef Kat, grab any interns you can see and forcibly drag them in here.

Kat has gone.

So. Where do we start? Rwandan genocide in 1994

Anne-Marie No we *cannot* start there.

Stef Alright, when the Belgians left in 1960

Anne-Marie We cannot start *there*

Stef Where do we start?

Anne-Marie Portugese arrive in Congo 1482

Stef Je / sus

Tony Fuck's sake

Anne-Marie Important because: Portugese say Kongo kingdom is well-developed.
Then (*claps*) everything change – sixteenth century, slave-traders

Stef We might need to jump forward

Anne-Marie Already this is a *white history* for you

Tony But we're talking about the problems *now* though.

Anne-Marie That's right. We *are*.
Slave-traders, first Portuguese then Dutch then you English then French, steal Congolais men to sell to work them to death.
Then comes Leopold.

Intern enters. Everyone turns to look at her.

Intern Kat said to come in here. (*Of Stef's face.*) Jesus, are you okay?

Stef could hand her a sheet of card and write 'L' on it – or some other visual aid.

Stef Fine. You are now King Leopold. You're a big Belgian with a beard and you never go to Africa but you own a huge bit of it. Stand on that chair which is Congo. Hold this.

51

Anne-Marie Congo Free State

Stef New name: write that, Intern.

Anne-Marie 1885 – Leopold takes rubber, uses forced labour. There is slaughter

Stef Ten million killed

Anne-Marie Fifteen million, more

Stef Well, numbers up in the air.

Anne-Marie Hands cut off

Stef Yep, amputation policy, for slow workers, Belgian officers *rewarded* for the number of hands they brought back.

Intern This is *horrible*.

Anne-Marie So first resource taken was men, then it was rubber, then palm oil.

Stef So, Tony, the line on Belgian colonialists is pretty clear.

Anne-Marie *Worst* colonial rule.

Tony Ever?

Stef Probably.

Anne-Marie Certainly.

Tony It's rare the Belgians are the best at anything

Stef (*to Anne-Marie*) Anything else?

Tony Chocolates. Arguably paedophilia.

Anne-Marie But not just the Belgians who benefit.

Stef The slave trade powers London, Bristol, Liverpool. Congo rubber for our bicycles, cars, industrial fan belts

Anne-Marie Congo copper drives your industrial revolution. Just like Congo minerals are drive China's / right now

Tony But sorry – the genocide in '94

Anne-Marie But that is *because* the colonialists make the Tutsi the favourite.

Kat enters.

Kat I can't find anyone else.

Tony Time?

Kat Two, three minutes at a push.

Stef Kat, can you come here and be the Tutsis, please. (*To Intern.*) And you're the Hutus.

Anne-Marie Colonial Europeans think Tutsi are better because they are taller and have more light skin.

Stef Swap!

The interns swap roles.

Anne-Marie Because Tutsi farm cow and are not nomadic, like Hutu.

Kat So I'm Hutu and I'm nomadic and I'm worse

Intern And I'm Tutsi and I've got cows

Stef Cows were everything, wealth, prestige, power – more protein.

Tony And why's this relevant?

Anne-Marie Europeans measure height, noses, skulls to see who is Hutu and Tutsi.

Stef Bigger skull bigger brain they thought.

Kat So the difference with Tutsi and Hutu is really more from Europe?

Stef You could even move between them. Before they were given racial ID cards.

Tony The Hutus and Tutsis were made into enemies by Europeans?

Anne-Marie Not quite so simple.

Stef But pretty much.

Tony Why don't I know about that?

Anne-Marie Who likes to learn the bad history?

Stef So jumping forward to Rwanda in '94 these tensions / erupted

Anne-Marie No. Congolese independence, 1960. Patrice Lumumba: the only truly elected leader of Congo.

Kat (*leaping up to be Lumumba*) What am I like?

Stef Great man – but

Anne-Marie The Mandela of our country – who the Americans killed before he could bring change.

Tony The Americans killed him?

Anne-Marie CIA and Belgian special forces. After three months in government

Stef Yes, look, he was really killed by the Belgians and the CIA with some Katangan / Congolese

Tony Not a conspiracy theory?

Stef No, they've admitted it

Tony Jesus wept.

Anne-Marie Killed for minerals – this time uranium

Intern Well, Lumumba's political naivety, wasn't it?

Anne-Marie Lumumba was a martyr for Congo and a true hero!

Intern Lumumba asked the Soviets for help: dead man walking.

Tony What do you know about it?

Intern I did History at LSE

Stef Some interns know a frightening amount

Intern My dissertation was / on Mobutu and Cold War proxy

Stef Except when to shut up.

Tony I do know a bit about Mobutu

Stef Tell us.

She gestures to Intern: 'Get up and be Mobutu.'

Tony Leopardskin tea cosy on his head, paid for the Rumble in the Jungle

Anne-Marie Renamed the country Zaire

Stef Relevance to today: he ruled for thirty-odd years, stole from the country and never improved the infrastructure.

Anne-Marie American puppet. They installed him.

Stef Well, they tolerated him

Intern Until I, Mobutu, lose American support under Clinton. I mean Bill. Obviously. Sorry.

Stef And then when the Rwandan Genocide happened in '94

Kat We really need to let them in.

Tony This is the bit I actually need!

Stef This is where I wanted to start!

Kat We'll stall them

She gestures to Intern to follow her. They leave.

Anne-Marie Listen – there is too much, *but*. After the genocide in '94, when huge numbers were displace into Congo. Many killers. And Rwanda chase the killers into Congo, slaughter many innocent people – which we never hear about. Mobutu is overthrown, by Kabila senior, father of the President now, all backed by Rwanda.

Stef Please be careful talking about Rwanda.

Tony The genocide?

Stef No, the country.

Anne-Marie The warmongering country – the Israel of the region.

Tony Oh so they're what – the only multicultural democracy?

Anne-Marie No, a small country with great aggression.

Stef (*to Tony*) D'you think we've got time to do the Middle East as well? Anne-Marie if you can bring yourself to be diplomatic about / Rwanda

Tony Quickly: bring me up to date.

Anne-Marie So now forty militias fight in the east, with Congo army just another militia. Phones, laptops, PlayStations drove the price of the minerals very high. That is why they fight.

Tony Coltan, right? What's / coltan?

Stef Oh / Jesus

Anne-Marie Coltan is columbite tantalum. So your phone can be so small and light. Thin dielectric layer. (*Shrugs.*) It's a superior element.

Tony Well, I see you have a science background.

Kat enters.

Kat We can't hold them any longer, we may lose people.

Stef Good luck, guys, I'll watch the live stream.

Tony Well, this hasn't been that helpful, but we'll get through it. Hold on. I'm bound to get asked about the rape, why is there so much rape?

Anne-Marie □
   Some think it's a way to express power passed down from colonial times.

Stef Militia near a mine will attack local villages and rape the women as a combat strategy.

Anne-Marie Mainly it's to break down the family. Destroy communities

Stef Because of ethnic rivalries, or to can gain access to the mine

Anne-Marie Yes. But it's also more than this.
   It's a problem everywhere. Twelve per cent of the Congolese women have been raped. It is normal. Not only in war. I was raped by my husband, before I left Congo. So. Many of us have had this.

   □

   ∎

Kat Sorry we. We do really need to let them in.

Stef touches Anne-Marie on the arm and leaves before the doors open.

57

EIGHT
THE LAUNCH

Conference room.
The press launch is near its end. Tony and Anne-Marie are seated on the raised platform.

Tony Thanks very much for listening. Maybe two more questions. Yes.

Luis slips in at the back of the room. Anne-Marie sees him, Tony does not.

Journalist 1 Anne-Marie, how much do you put the troubles of Congo down to Rwandan interference?

Tony Obviously tensions with Rwanda exist. But it's incredibly important a festival like ours is allowed to make a positive contribution, raising awareness without providing easy answers for a complex problem.

Journalist 1 Thank you, but I did direct that to Anne-Marie.

Anne-Marie All Congolese have opinions about the problems at home. But this festival is not about my opinion.

Tony Absol—

Anne-Marie But Rwanda is a big problem.

Tony Absol— Uh, yeah. One more question.

Luis How do you react to the idea that this festival is betraying millions of dead in Congo?

Tony I'd say you're wrong and I'd say I didn't point to you for last question

Luis Because of this British Parliament, who back the criminals of Rwanda and Congo governments?

Anne-Marie I don't know how this man get in here. He is part of a violent group called Les Combattants.

Luis I have press accreditation.

Anne-Marie From?

Tony Alright, let's move / on

Luis AfricanBugle website.

Anne-Marie It doesn't exist.

Luis Check the website.

Tony Okay, last question, over here?

Luis You not take questions from Congolese?

Tony Not from you, fella, you're in a pressure group that makes death threats. Don't act all surprised about it.

Luis Strange strange ideas.

Tony Let's draw things to a close. Thanks for listening.

Luis You listen to nothing – this is the way with your white festival.

Anne-Marie You shame Congo. I want security to take them out.

Tony I'm sure it's not necessary.

Anne-Marie No, I want security please.

The security man on the door speaks into his radio and approaches Luis.

Luis Wait. <This you will regret>

Anne-Marie I don't feel comfort with violent criminals in here. Security please.

Luis cooperates with security, but continues speaking with force.

Luis The press have to know that this woman supports the criminal government of Congo. Like dem she silence any voice against her!

Anne-Marie I do not! I just do not support you!

Luis is gone.

Tony Alright, let's slip that last question in shall we? Yup.

Journalist 2 Is Congo for you a story of – sorry to be reductive but – a story of globalisation in which mineral wars, for our technology, are the main cause of the conflict and the rapes?

Tony Uh, Anne-Marie?

Anne-Marie For me Congo is not a story. It is a place. People live in it. People like you and me but who are never safe and is not their fault. Women most of all. But if Congo *is* a story, it must be the worst story in history. Because no one ever wants to hear it.

Tony Mmm, absolutely. It's worth mentioning Congo has long been exploited for its resources whether that be rubber or palm oil, right back to Portuguese slave traders in the fifteenth century.

He looks briefly smug.

Thank you. Any further questions can be sent to Stephanie Cartwright whose email is at the bottom of the press release.

Outside Westminster tube station. Stef is typing on her smartphone.

Oudry Successful press launch of Hashtag CongoVoice Fest. We guarantee Congolese voices in our decisions. Any Congolese interested contact ASAP.

Tony and Anne-Marie enter.

Stef Well done well done. The live stream was really clear. You both dealt with everything brilliantly.

Anne-Marie Thank you.

Stef I can't believe the main guy from Les Combattants managed to get in.

Anne-Marie Luis. His name is Luis.

Tony Should we all perhaps go for a drink?

Anne-Marie I must go to my father.

Stef Of course.

Anne-Marie leaves them.

Tony Can you believe what she told us, before the launch?

Stef The problem is, Tony, that I can.

□

Tony What do you want to do now?

Stef I dunno. Cry.

Tony Why?

Stef I dunno.
□
Will you kiss me?

■

Tony I shouldn't, I mean

■

Stef No, you're right of course.

Tony Yes. I will.

Stef No, you're right.

Tony I will. I'd like to.

Stef No, you're absolutely right, it would've solved nothing.

Tony It could've been nice.

Stef No, it would've solved nothing.
I'm gonna go and try to wash this stuff off.

Stef kisses him on the cheek and is about to leave.

Thank you. For today. Tomorrow we make a start on the acts.

Tony Well. Good luck.

Stef And you're not coming.

Tony I said I'd help with the press launch.

Stef Yes.

Tony Not book the

Stef No.

Tony ■
Although

Stef Yes?

Tony What time tomorrow?

Stef Just pop your head in at eleven.

Tony Stef? Are you absolutely sure?

Stef It can be midday / if you want

Tony You know what I mean.

Stef I do.

Tony gestures to the red on her face.

Tony This whole. Today. Are you absolutely sure it's worth it?

Stef I am actually.
Yes.

She leaves.

NINE
DOCTOR CHICKENBONES

A hut in a village in South Kivu, East DRC.
Oudry (no hat) plays his thumb-piano by the bed of his daughter Patience, about twelve.

Patience <Another song!>

Oudry <It's too late for music now.>

Patience <When can I have a thumb-piano of my own to play?>

Oudry <Well, when I die I will give you this.>

Patience <I don't want you to die.>

Oudry <No, but my spirit will join with the spirit in this object. Because I made it.>

Patience <How about a story?>

Oudry <Your mother's waiting for me to come to bed.>

Patience <She's not, she's drinking next door with Mama Salima.>

Oudry □
<You notice too much.>

Patience <Please.>

Oudry <Your brothers are back tomorrow.>

Patience <So?>

Oudry <You need to sleep so you can help feed them.>

Patience <If I go to sleep, tomorrow will you give me a beer?>

Oudry <If it's a good week, they'll bring some. Goodnight.>

He leans in to kiss her, she ignores him.

<What sort of ungrateful child are you?>

Patience <Please one, a short one.>

Oudry <You've heard them all before. Just remember one and tell it to yourself>

Patience <Why don't I tell you one> So I can practise, for my own children>

Oudry <What do you mean, practise?>

Patience <I mean. No>

Oudry <What do you mean, practise?>

Patience <No, I didn't mean. I mean so I can get as good as you.>

Oudry <Because if you have a child now you know where it's going.>

Patience turns away from him and buries her head.

<Unless its father is a prince. Or a trader.
    Then you know where it's going.
    Maybe you've met a trader? If you've met a trader, don't keep it to yourself.>

■ *Oudry gets up to go. He sits back down.*

<You'll have babies one day, when you are paired and things are easier.>

        ■

<Alright tell me a story, tell me a *short* one.>

   Patience bounces back up.

Patience <Ha, great, which one is short?>

Oudry <I am too soft, seriously.>

Patience <How about 'Why the crocodile wouldn't eat
the hen?'>

Oudry <No, no, far too long.>

Patience <The television singer who went to Europe.>

Oudry <That's *much* too long.>

Patience <It's fun though>

Oudry <And it's not a good story for a child.>

Patience <Well, I'm not a child so that's fine>

Oudry <No.>

Patience <'The wasp who ate his own face'?>

Oudry <I never told you this story.>

Patience <No, I made it up.>

Oudry <Strange, crazy child.>

Patience <'The kind brothers who came back from the
mine with a necklace for Patience.'>

Oudry <Alright now>

Patience <And beer.>

Oudry <Alright now, I'm going to bed.>

Patience <No no, a short one. 'Doctor ChickenBones
who saved lives and ate babies.' Please?
   And after I'll fall straight asleep.
   Probably before the end even.>

Oudry <That is a short one. Go on then.>

Patience <Okay. This story is called 'Doctor ChickenBones who saved – (*yawns*) lives and ate'>

She pretends to fall suddenly deeply asleep. Oudry gets up to walk out.
Patience springs up.

<'Babies.' Well. Many years ago, many many years before I was born.
  Or my brother Cedric was born.
  Or my brother Ben.
  Or Mama Beatrice was born. Or>

Oudry <Stop it.>

Patience <What?>

Oudry <You're making it longer.>

Patience <That's just how I remember it, Papa.>

Oudry <Did someone give you sugar water? In the Long Ago. This story is set in the Long Ago anyway.>

Patience <In the Long Ago there was a man who used to dress in white clothes which never became muddy. He was a doctor and he would save many lives. But he liked to eat babies. And so he did.>

Oudry <He *needed* to eat babies to stay alive.>

Patience <Did he not like eating them as well?>

Oudry <Do you like everything you eat?>

Patience <Not when it's left it in the pot for three days.>

Oudry slaps her.

Oudry <Your mother is a good cook.>

Patience <Yes I'm sorry, Papa, it was a joke.>

Oudry <Continue.>

Patience <Doctor ChickenBones was a good doctor and when mothers came to him, he would help their babies be born healthy.

But if he saw a mother would not love her baby, he would choose this baby to be eaten. Then he would tell the mother that it was a spirit had taken the baby. And the doctor would throw all the little bones in a pile and say they were chicken bones.

So everyone came to call him Doctor ChickenBones.

One day a woman came to the doctor and gave birth to a baby that was very strange and weak. This mother was very sad, but she loved her baby.

Doctor ChickenBones was so hungry that he took it away and ate it anyway. It tasted very, very good.

The mother was so upset she carved a wooden figure, a Nkishi with a straw headdress, for a spirit to live inside.

When she asked the spirit why it took her baby, it did not reply.

Instead the Nkishi waited until Doctor ChickenBones went on a long walk to look for herbs. Papa, how far do Cedric and Ben walk in one day?>

Oudry <They walk as far as they can get in daylight.>

Patience <Where do Cedric and Ben take the rocks?>

Oudry <Any reason to stay awake, isn't it.>

Patience <Do they go to Bukavu?>

Oudry <Yes, you can ask them about this>

Patience <How far normally?>

Oudry <It changes. It's about how many rocks the miners find, and how many the commander takes. Ask your brothers about it tomorrow. When you've *slept.*>

Patience <Don't you know about it?>

Oudry <Of course I know about it. I used to work there.

67

The story of how Papa grew too tall for the mine but not broad enough to carry rocks.>

Patience <There's something special inside the rocks, Cedric says.>

Oudry <I'm told that goes to Rwanda.>

Patience <And then after that.>

Oudry <It's sold. Things are made with it.>

Patience <And will they use it to build a tunnel from here to Europe?>

Oudry <No no, this rock will go to America to help rebuild the two towers.>

Patience <Two towers?>

Oudry <They are two enormous towers in a city that were smashed one day by crazy pilots.>

Patience <I never heard of that.>

Oudry <I saw television of it in Bukavu. Amazing, the tall towers falling to the ground on fire, it was very beautiful actually.>

Patience <And that's where the rock goes, to build two towers smashed by crazy pilots?>

Oudry <Yes, I dunno, that's what people say, am I in America?>

Patience <I'd love to meet an American.>

Oudry <Huh.>

Patience <Maybe tomorrow you can tell me the story of the two towers?>

Oudry <It's not a story, there is no story, two planes hit two towers. They fell down. I don't know anything else.>

Patience <When?>

Oudry <Lord! Just before you were born – *finish!*>

Patience <The Nkishi followed Doctor ChickenBones into the forest, and called out to him, 'Oh Doctor, is it you who has eaten all the babies?' And Doctor ChickenBones was so angry that he struck the Nkishi But his hand became fixed to the Nkishi.
'Let go or I will hit you with my other hand,' said ChickenBones.
But the Nkishi said, 'Oh Doctor, it *is* you who has eaten all the babies.'
And ChickenBones struck with his other hand and that too became fixed to the Nkishi.
Without both hands, Doctor ChickenBones could not catch anything to eat. And soon he was starving.
'Why not eat your own tongue if you are hungry?' said the Nkishi.
And ChickenBones was so hungry that he did, he bit off his own tongue and ate it. And finally his white clothes which never became dirty were covered in blood. It was not his blood but the blood of the babies that he had eaten. And his mouth which ate all the babies became so full of the blood that he never breathed again and fell down dead. And that's the end of the story.>

Oudry <Good, you know it quite well.>

Patience <Thank you.>

Oudry <And you do listen.
Of course you know Nkishi can't do those things.>

Patience <Of course. But did people used to think that way?>

There are yells in the distance. Oudry is suddenly alert. They listen.
More yells. They listen again. They look at each other.

■

69

*Oudry springs up and grabs food. He pulls Patience
out of bed by her arm; it hurts her. He grabs a T-shirt,
wraps food in it and presses it into her stomach.*

\<Run for the bush. Don't come back for two days.\>

More yells and voices outside.
  *The door of the hut opens. They look up. Beatrice
runs in.*

Patience \<Mama.\>

Oudry \<Is it? Is it!\>

Beatrice \<It's the Commander's men. Patience, run now!\>

*Patience looks at her mother, then her father, and runs
out of the door.*

Oudry \<And you too.\>

*There are more yells, growing nearer. Beatrice is
scrabbling for food, Oudry helping her. Beatrice turns
to run out of the door.*
  *A man forces his way in. He is a Militiaman, tall
and raggedly dressed, a Kalashnikov slung casually
over his shoulder.*
  He stands looking at them.
  *Oudry and Beatrice start throwing all their food and
possessions in front of him.*

Beatrice \<There you go, there you go, take it all.\>

*The man stands still. He looks at them. There are now
loud screams and gunshots in the near distance.*
  Another man enters holding Patience.

\<She is diseased, she is diseased!\>

The men laugh. One of them points his rifle at Oudry.

Militiaman \<You are first.\>

TEN
ELECTRIC THINGS

The same hut. Next morning.
   The noise of people busy outside. Patience sits with her legs tightly in front of her chest.
   Meredith is sitting next to Patience with a notepad. Meredith is a Canadian in the uniform of an international medical charity.
   Between the brackets, Meredith speaks falteringly in a language she is not fluent in.

■

■

Meredith <I look, quick look, I help.>

■

Patience shakes her head.

<Your mother. I look.
   Before. I help your mother.>

■

<True.>

■ *Meredith goes to her and looks at her hair.*

<May I touch?>

Patience thinks and nods. Meredith strokes her hair.
   Patience slightly loosens her hands in front of her knees. Meredith very delicately parts Patience's legs and inspects her wounds. It is very quick.

<Thank you very much. We help you.>

Meredith hands Patience some water, takes out a radio and stands up to leave.

<I go, short time. Not far.>

71

Patience shakes her head. She looks imploringly at Meredith.

■

<You not alone.>

Patience begins to get upset.

<Patience, speak English?>

Patience shakes her head slightly. Meredith sits down. And takes out a radio.

Okay, so can you understand what I'm saying *now*? If I'm speaking English do you understand me? Anything?

Patience □

Meredith Okay, fine. <I stay.>

Patience is happier. Meredith reads into radio in a deliberately calm and clear voice.

Receiving? Over.

Girl thirteen fourteen, mother maybe late thirties. Two brothers work at the tin mine, meant to return today, haven't yet. Father machete wound to head, some scalp missing, broken nose and eye swollen shut. Fortuitous walking wounded. Wife raped by two men. Daughter by six including probable forced assault by father. Probable EB2. Suspected insertion of bayonet. Fistula. Severe bleeding stemmed by improvised rag. Recommend PEP kit. Over.

Radio Can mother walk, over?

Meredith Just about, over.

Radio Send to clinic, treat only emergencies on ground, over.

Meredith Received, over.

Radio Daughter emergency, over?

Meredith Daughter emergency yes, over.

Meredith puts the radio down and sits with Patience.

■

■

<Patience. I need go now.>

Patience screws up her face.

<I go help more people>

A noise outside. Patience becomes agitated.
Someone is entering.
It is Stef. She is extremely panicked.

Wh—
Don't

Stef Sorry.

Meredith Don't come in. Don't come any further in.

Stef Sorry sorry, I

Meredith It's fine, just

Stef I didn't know this was

Meredith Just stay put.
<Patience? This my friend. She kind.>
□
Okay so.
You're the Brit they left.

Stef Yeah. Stef.

Meredith Okay you need to speak very calmly, Stef.
To me, not to her.
No sudden movements.
What is it?

Stef The sat phone has started working.

Meredith Okay.

Stef Um, I. I don't. Someone told me to just get the sat phone working.
   I don't know what to do next.

Meredith Sure

Stef I don't wanna waste the –

Meredith Sure.

Stef – sat phone battery. And you're the nearest. What's this called?

Meredith A hut.

Stef A hut, oh yeah.

Meredith Take the sat phone. And walk back to the four-by-fours.

Stef There's a man outside with a hole in his head.

Meredith And sit in the four-by-fours

Stef What about the man?

Meredith He's being dealt with.

Stef He's not

Meredith He is.

Stef He's not, I promise.

Meredith He is *being*. Dealt with. If there's no one with him that doesn't

Stef There isn't

Meredith That doesn't mean he's not being dealt with. Please calm down

   Patience has become agitated at the tone.

74

(*To Patience.*) <Now good. Now safe.>

Stef Okay yeah.

Meredith They brought you for your hands. But not here okay.

Stef Okay, wh—
What about my hands?

Meredith Use your hands on the sat phone. In the four-by-four.
That is where you're gonna be most helpful. Yes?

Stef Yes.

Meredith Call the last dialled number. And report the co-ordinates on the display.
Well done. You're doing a great job.

Stef So are you

Meredith Okay thanks but. Just. Walk back now. Walk back to the four-by-fours.

Stef Yes. I'm going.

Meredith Don't look at the man.

Stef It's a terrible wound.

Meredith Don't look at the wound. What're you not gonna do?

Stef I'm not gonna look.

Meredith One foot in front of the other. Go and get it done.

Stef leaves.

<I'm sorry, my friend wants to help.>

☐

■

Patience <She was talking then about the rocks?>

□

Meredith <Sorry, again?>

Patience <You are here for the rocks?>

Meredith Uh
<Sorry, I don't understand. 'Ro—'?>

Patience <The rocks from the mine.>

Meredith <Rocks?>
Oh right yeah
<No, I not here rocks from the mine, I here to help
you.>

Patience <Are they to build your two towers the rocks?>

Meredith <Towers, no the rocks don't build towers.>

Patience <Oh.>

Meredith <The rocks build other things.
Electric things.>

*Patience doesn't understand. Meredith leans in to help
her.*

ELEVEN
MORE HELP IS

Outside the hut.
   *Oudry sits slumped and dazed. A dressing flapping
from a recent head wound.*
   Blood and scalp visible.
   Stef leaves the hut. She is shaken and unsteady.
   *She walks with purpose past Oudry, not looking at
him.*

Stef I'm sorry. More help is.
I can't.

■

She stops suddenly, she has stepped on something.
She picks it up. It is his thumb-piano. She holds it
out to him without looking at him.

I'm sorry, I have to walk to the four-by-fours.

She nearly looks at him.
Oudry takes it. In taking it from her, a note is half
played.

I'm told to walk back to the four-by-fours.

Stef moves past him and exits without looking at him.

■

End of Part One.

Part Two

TWELVE
FOUND POETRY

Oudry is different from Part One. He no longer has a hat on and his wound is visible. His relationship with the audience has changed – he plays up to them more. His relationship with Stef has changed – he is a distraction to her. He invades scenes. He plays music.

*

The act opens with a burst of sustained song from a rumba band. It is exuberant and energising. It could start in the interval.

Stef and Tony are visible, watching a video of the band on a tablet.

Tony stops it on the tablet and the band stops.

Tony What these guys've got going for them is they'd appeal to the Congolese here *and* the polo-necks who buy world music.

Stef Oh, they're wonderful. Do they have political affiliations in Congo?

Tony They've performed public concerts that politicians attended, but that's it.

Stef So this is the band.

Tony Yeah, I really think so.

Stef Tony?

Tony Yes?

Stef Well done.

Tony Thank you.

I did find this one lot – they do rumba covers of western indie rock.

Tony swipes his tablet and the band burst out one line of 'Heaven Knows I'm Miserable Now' by The Smiths in an upbeat rumba style. Stef swipes it away.

Stef Yeah, great fun, but they're obviously not all Congolese and they're not right for the festival.
Have you had time to look at these poems?

Tony takes her tablet and scans the poem. Victor enters and watches as they read.

Oudry
Inside my ten-inch netbook
thunderheads forming in clusters on the squall line
worldviews are exchanged
used to solder a circuit board that
approved pharmacy medicines
shaped by lack of editorial care
shipped direct to where they're needed
ensure Zenith Bank can help you
when your battery goes dead
and lose memory of those happy times
local slappers waiting by their phones
children asking at the window for pens
allowing the viewer to detach themselves.

□

Stef It's just

□

Tony Personally I don't understand how they're poems.

Stef I think we do understand how they're poems, but we

Victor Yes?

Stef We don't necessarily see them as something compatible with the festival.

79

Victor It is Congolese poetry.

Oudry enters the scene (or interacts with it in a way he hasn't before). Stef's eye is drawn by him.

Stef It's not, it's not *recognisably* part of a uh, a Congolese tradition, is it?

Victor It's Congolese.

Tony Sure

Victor It's written by a Congolese.

Stef For the festival to be a truly awareness-raising event, we need the submissions to reflect Congo.

Victor These reflect Congo, very closely.
    It's poems put together by a person from emails.
    From spam emails. Sent by people he never met. And he takes the words. And makes it into a poem.

Tony So the poet didn't write it?

Victor He did not write the words but he did write the poem.

Tony So it's a cut'n'paste job.

Victor He took these emails as raw materials, they don't belong to him, and he changed them around to be something else, that belong to him.

Stef is trying not to be distracted by Oudry.

Stef I suppose I think that, if you have to take time explaining that then, then I wonder how valuable that is.

Victor People do it very much, very frequently.

Stef Do they?

Victor It's called 'found poetry'.

Stef I'm sorry I didn't study literature.

Victor But I did, you see.

*Oudry produces an mbira (thumb-piano) from
somewhere within the scene. The framed sick bag?
A tablet becoming an mbira? Could be a larger version
of the one she saw him with in Scene Nine and Eleven.*

Stef Could we meet the poet?

■

Victor Why is this important?

Stef Victor, can I ask. Are we meeting the poet right now?

Victor ■
Why don't you ask Anne-Marie to read the poems? She
would read them very beautifully, I think.

Stef I suppose what we want to ask is – had the poet
thought about writing something more, something more
directly about the problems of your, his country?

Oudry plays some notes on the mbira.

Victor You want me to ask him to try again?

Stef Could you? Ask him to write more, uh, directly.
About DRC.

Victor □
I can see.

Tony Thanks, Victor.

Stef We really appreciate your input, whether we can use
these poems or not – you're coming to the committee
meeting on Friday?

Victor Yes. You need your one-third, don't you?

Stef Sure but. It's also important to me.

Victor exits.

*Stef is alone. Oudry looks at Stef and engages with her
in a new way. Perhaps he smiles broadly at her for the*

*first time and holds her gaze. Whatever it is, it is a
strange disconcerting moment for her.*

*She concentrates on her tablet. Oudry reads to her
and plays his thumb-piano.*

Oudry
My telephone contains
soaring yellow-beaked birds
in campus novel form,
is life mouthwatering lobster-tail
a routine opening hatches responding to signals
chatting and meeting nice new friend
nobody applies to claim money
we photograph their dead in different ways
nobody now looks for answers past
a bold move beyond market failure
can make her understand you
need to be as slim as a cavewoman
finally free from shame
soaked in cosmoline packing grease
browsing in a mode that will not record your history.

Stand-up Oliver enters and prepares to do his act.

(*Plays a note.*) Next: Oliver, British-Congolese comedian.

Oliver 'Any Ugandans in? No, okay, perfect! I use to
date a Ugandan girl.' Then the crowd is like, ahhh I
dunno what I think about that. And I go
  'But I had to stop because this girl, you've never met a
girl like her. First time I take her for a date, whenever I
stop the car she is always kissing me. Then I take her
home and park outside her house, and she put my hand
straight between her legs. Straight between!'
  Then the crowd is like, eeeeh.
  'And she is like this, oh yeah oh yeah oh Oliver – she
remembered my name eh'
  Laugh.

And then, 'Please are you married?' 'No, why do you ask?' 'Because the ring on your finger is hurting me!' And I say, 'That is not a ring, that is my wristwatch.' Beeg laugh.

'Swiss-made Tag Heuer original, and I'm going home now because I don't want to lose it!' Another laugh, less but still good.

□

Tony Great

Stef Yeah. Great

Oliver So yeah, that's something, uh. For the late-night crowd, late-night but very good response.

Ira enters, a formidable African American writer.

Oudry (*plays a note*) Ira Coleman, American writer.

Ira (*reads*)
That night.
Men approached the camp.
Their faces were steel.
Their hands were bruised fruit.
They would shut out the moon.

Tony and Stef with Ira.

Tony So powerful.

Stef Wow. The momentum of the writing.

Ira Thank you. I was blessed to interview a number of strong Congolese women. I was just trying to do them justice.

Stef Where did you interview them?

Ira Anywhere. Rooms, kitchens, the street.

Stef In Congo?

Ira Uh, no, these were in communes in Uganda or people who'd sought asylum in the US.

Stef Right.

Ira Yeah.

Tony What we've got is a spot for a reading.

Stef So did you get to go to Congo in the end?

Ira I went to Africa twice for this book.

Stef To Congo?

Ira Is it a problem if I didn't?

Tony No, not at all, of course not, I've never been.

Ira You have though, right?

Oudry reacts. He could play a series of sharp notes.

Stef Visiting to observe a medical charity but ended up a bit more. Involved.

Ira Of course it's a conflict that politicians really don't understand. Because it's a gender war waged not on land but on women's bodies.

Stef Yes, although it is hard to ignore the infrastructure, the economics, the history.

Ira I didn't ask you to ignore anything.

□

Stef I mean, I don't know how much of a traditional feminist reading I'd take on it.

Ira You don't *know*?

■

Tony Ira, is there a story of yours you think would suit the festival?

84

Ira Sorry, could you finish your point.

Stef I had finished it.

Ira Oh that's funny because, well it seems a very unfinished point to me.

Stef I'd be reluctant to view it purely through a uh, a gender theory filter.

Ira What context do you want to view the wholesale targeting and destruction of one gender in a society?
What's that, is that to do with the weather?
Is that climatology maybe?

Tony Ha, okay – it's divisive isn't it. Is there

Ira You tell me. What filter do I look at it from?

Tony and Stef, later. Ira is gone.

Tony You didn't back me up at all!

Stef I couldn't, Tony, I couldn't do it

Tony She's gonna pull out I guarantee it, she hated you

Stef Well. Mutual.

Tony Didn't realise my booking criteria included 'no women Stef might feel threatened by'.

Stef Threatened!

Tony Look at that seminar leader at SOAS, you turned all the others against her cos you took her on in class and she won.

Stef □
You've never met them. That's.
How could you possibly know about that?

Tony You must've mentioned it. Carmen Lankena's here in two minutes

Stef I've never mentioned that.

Tony A photo from Carmen will sort the visual identity for your whole festival

Stef Tony, how do you know all this stuff about my life?

Tony I don't.

Stef You're freaking me out.

Tony This is an important meeting now

Stef It's been five times you've known stuff about me you could only know by. What? Stalking?

Tony No, look, no

Stef Private detective?

Tony The reason I.
　No.

Stef So there *is* a reason, I'm not out of my mind?

Tony ■
　The reason I know is. I did an unacceptable thing.

Stef Like what?

Tony Like.
　Like I had your email password for about a year after we broke up.

Stef Oh.

　　■

Fucking hell that's. That's horrible Tony that's really fucking horrible.

Tony Well so is sending an email to Cassey laughing at my bent cock.

Stef Sorry, *what*?

Tony I've read it. Your email to Cassey laughing at my bent cock.

Stef I wasn't laughing *at* it.

Tony Oh what were you doing, laughing *with* it? Laughing *with* my bent cock.

Stef It was affection, it was affectionate, I used to love. The time we had.

☐

You don't even have that / bent a cock!

Tony Bit late now after comparing it to an Aboriginal throwing weapon.

Oudry (*plays a note*) Carmen Lankena, photographer.

Carmen Lankena enters, a glamorous American photographer.

Tony Carmen. Hi! We're chuffed you came.

Carmen Chuffed? I'm chuffed too. What a great word. Chuff also means vagina doesn't it?

☐

Stef Not in this context but. Can do.

Carmen Well, I'm vagina'd to be here. Thank God you're not the normal pious NGO pricks. Jeez, I'm up to my eyes in it. Talk to me.

Stef I think we can both say, with total honestly, we find your photos quite brilliant.

Carmen Thank you, that's so kind.

Tony I've known her a long time and I know when she means it.

Stef The photos really make you look at the people as people, not poor people in a bad place. Not victims, not *the other*. Even the soldiers we see as people.

Tony For the campaign, if you could think, of allowing us to use one or even two

Carmen Oh no. No no.
  You can use all of them.
  However you like. I'll tell my people – all reproduction issues waived.

Stef That is quite outstandingly generous!

Tony But. We should tell you. There have been death threats.

Carmen Pfff. How bad can it be?

  □

Tony Well at worst, death I suppose.

Carmen They'd do very well to kill me. I spend most of my life on aeroplanes.
  Listen, I took a load of photos. It's the worst place I ever been. I felt shitty. I mostly felt shitty talking to people about changing their situation, filling 'em up with hope, and then gone again in an instant. So I'm pretty desperate not to make any money out of those photos.
  Then I'd feel *really* bad.
  Tell you what, have them exclusively.
  This is addictive, isn't it?

Stef Are you serious?

Carmen Oh, as an atrocity.

Stef The photos will make a world of difference. Thank you.

Carmen My pleasure. My relief actually.

Carmen exits.
Tony looks to Stef to celebrate. Stef is still angry.

Tony All I did was *not* forget the password. I have a very good memory.

Stef Does trust mean anything to you?

Tony I never had a fund named after it.

Oliver continues.

Oliver I have a bit where I am a traffic warden. He's basically Nigerian but I don't say, I go: 'Only de other day, I say to a man "Eh, you cannot park dere, dat is a disabled space, what is your disability?" and he say, "I've got Tourette's and you can fuck off."'

That is late-night gold.

I have bits that are very clean also, but that is real gold stuff.

Oudry plays his thumb-piano. He is enjoying himself.

Oudry Welcome and thank you all new followers to hashtag CongoVoice campaign. Check out our exciting festival acts here: tickets already selling fast.

THIRTEEN
HANDS GO UP

The meeting room in Portcullis House, same as Scene Six. Stef, Tony, Anne-Marie, Victor, Jenny, Fred and Alice. Oudry bored, idly toying with his mbira.

Stef Before we start, may I briefly welcome Alice Ekofu from the new organisation DRC Horizon. Alice was born in DRC but came here at three years old and recently graduated from the same college *and* course as me. She's just started her own organisation to help Congo and without piling pressure on her, I think in Alice we have a real example of a new generation of British Congolese engaging with the country's future.

Alice Thank you, I'm very new to this so, any help would be amazing.

Stef Welcome to the team, Alice.

She smiles at her, then smiles at Jenny.
Samo enters late and waves an apology.

Hi, Samo. Now before I ask Tony to report on some exciting festival developments, we must vote once more on / the constitution

Jenny You haven't updated us on the press launch, Stephanie.

Stef No, true. Well I think the press launch went off very well. The live / stream was

Jenny You had an issue with hosting it? You called me.

Stef I did, I was indisposed on the day.

Anne-Marie shoots a look at Stef. Oudry shows his displeasure. Tony is unsure.

But Tony stepped in and did admirably.

Anne-Marie A little more than indisposed.

Jenny But you're feeling better?

Stef Raring to go, Jenny. (*Looks at her tablet.*) So, the constitution.

Oudry (*sings*) Vote: CongoVoice campaign will tolerate no explicit political statements.

Jenny This is a formality I think.

Fred Yep, very important, to have any credibility.

Stef Obviously Parliament won't have it and we'll get nowhere with a divisive agenda, shall we vote?

Victor But the problem of the country *is* political. How can we not have political statements?

Alice There's no way to comment on this situation without intrinsic political content.

Stef Ah.

Samo It is absolutely standard for a campaign like this.

Alice We can't even say the President stole the election?

Fred None of us are political organisations.

Alice We are.

Jenny With respect, you're barely an organisation. Are you even a registered charity?

Alice We're registering, but that's not the point I'm making

Jenny Well, the point we're making is that without Parliament we might as well all give up, go home and write angry blogs

Alice Maybe I will because at least I won't be silenced.

Stef You can write blogs, just separately of CongoVoice.

Alice This is a festival to help Congo which can't say what's wrong with Congo.

Fred Such is the job.

Alice You say this festival can give Congolese a voice. But you police how they use that voice. I can't believe my tutor told me I might be on board with this. Sorry, but. We're out.

Stef Alice, this seems like a big thing

Alice I have my own campaign, I don't need to swallow your compromises.

Fred We all swallow our fair share

Alice (*to Stef*) You're gonna lose a lot of the Congolese youth this way. I'm sorry but that's just true.

She leaves. Oudry watches her go and looks back at Stef.

Jenny We're already less than one-third. What now?

Stef We count Alice's vote as a no, it's still passed. No more votes today – next meeting we'll make sure we have one-third.

Oudry reacts.

Jenny Next meeting, of course.

Stef Tony, update us on the acts.

Tony If it's only a third, couldn't we, I mean

Jenny Yes?

Tony Couldn't one of the whites just walk out?

Samo Of the non-Congolese

Jenny You could, Tony, but the festival needs our financial pledges.

Fred And just you would still leave only two out of seven, less than a third.

Oudry reacts – musically? Physically?

Stef Just update us on the acts, Tony.

Tony Firstly I'm sorry to say that Ira Coleman the writer can no longer play a role in the festival.

Anne-Marie Ira Coleman! That is a sadness.

Tony She has a. *Clash*. (*Looks at Stef.*)

Anne-Marie She is the best writer about Congo.

Stef Ira Coleman, really?

Anne-Marie You are surprised?

Victor Who did you think – Le Carré?

Stef D'you like Ira Coleman, Victor?

Victor She's okay, sentimental.

> *Stef's tablet is being passed around with photos on it.*
> *Oudry could be following it, and looking at it over*
> *people's shoulders, clowning, sharing his reaction with*
> *the audience. Stef is trying not to be distracted by him.*

Tony The good news is: we have secured the permission
to *exclusively* use the photographs of Eastern Congo
taken by Carmen Lankena.

Jenny Well done. That's very classy.

Samo Very very good.

Fred That's a coup. I mean the right sort of coup.

> *Anne-Marie is being handed the tablet.*

Stef Does everyone know Carmen's work?

Anne-Marie No.

Tony I think you'll really like it

Anne-Marie No, you cannot use this, it is terrible.

> *Anne-Marie passes the tablet to Victor. Oudry is*
> *perturbed.*

Stef Why?

Victor <What's wrong with it? Oh Lord.>
No you cannot use this.

Jenny I thought they were deeply sympathetic.

Victor Do you know how were they taken?

Tony Like, what lens?

Anne-Marie She is with a foreign army.

Oudry is traumatised at this. He shakes his head. Stef clocks him.

Stef Oh.

Tony Meaning?

Victor This uniform, at the back

Stef Oh dear.

Victor This photographer enter East Congo with a neighbouring army.

Anne-Marie Embedded, embedded is the English word.

Tony Why's it bad?

Victor People will say this is photos taken by an *invading force*.

Samo The Congolese government invite African countries to help.

Anne-Marie Against the will of the people.

Stef My fault, hadn't thought it through. We can't use the photos.

Tony Can we talk about it?

Anne-Marie We talked about it. No.

Stef is looking directly at Oudry.

Stef We *can't*. Moving on. Oliver the comedian?

Jenny We can pretty much all agree on that.

Samo Are we worried about political statements?

Tony We're not

Stef We're almost certainly not.

Tony He doesn't do politics, it's mainly about Ugandan women being loose.

Samo About what?

Everyone realises and looks at Samo.
☐

Tony Oh God.

Samo Loose?

Victor Like uh, easy.

Tony That's one routine.

Samo Easy how?

Jenny All comedians take liberties.

Victor Easy to uh, easy to have sex with – it's an idiom: 'she's *loose*'.

Tony He can leave that out

Anne-Marie It's terrible stereotyping

Samo Ugandan women are never 'easy'.

Anne-Marie But sometimes true.

Victor It's actually his best material.

Tony He'll do the stuff about his mum.
And finally, the jewel in the crown of the evening, this band.

Tony passes round the tablet with a video of the band. The band play and it blasts out a full sound.

Oudry Today hashtag CongoVoice received its five thousandth follower. Keep abreast of festival updates on the go.

Later. Stef finishes watching the band on her tablet and closes it. The band stop. Anne-Marie enters.

Stef Thank you for being there. Those meetings should be the easy bit. They're always the hardest.

Anne-Marie 'Indisposed'. What is this meeting-mouth language you have. You were attacked.

Stef A lot of this stuff is about momentum. They don't need to know.

Anne-Marie Stephanie.

Stef I don't want to give the Combattants the satisfaction.

Anne-Marie But of course you've reported to the police?

Oudry is interested to hear Stef's answer.

Stef ■
Anne-Marie, if I reported that incident

Anne-Marie Attack

Stef If I reported it I think Huw Bennion would find a way to ease me off the festival.

Anne-Marie Why?!

Stef Because he'd get spooked and make me take a holiday and give my job to Jenny Walton from Human Rights Monitor.

Anne-Marie Are you sure he would do that?

Stef And she's an NGO careerist with no vision. And she will drop our promise of one-third Congolese. And she's never even *been*.

Anne-Marie You are being paranoid.

Oudry Don't look at the wound.

Stef's head snaps towards him and back to Anne-Marie, shaken.

Stef I'm not, Anne-Marie, trust me this is how these things work.

Anne-Marie If you don't report it, you are saying it's acceptable and next time it will be worse.

Stef It washed off, okay, it wasn't very nice but getting the police involved will harm the festival. Wouldn't it be better if I go and talk to them / myself?

Anne-Marie Les Combattants? Save your breath.

Stef Well, I've organised a meeting for tomorrow. They've directly threatened the band we've booked and I've got to deal with it.

Oudry approves.

Anne-Marie They have threated the band now?

Stef Don't worry, I'm meeting them in public. An internet café in Turnpike Lane.

Anne-Marie You and Tony?

Stef No. I haven't told him. I'm going alone.

Anne-Marie □
This is not personal. Why do you make it personal?

Stef and Oudry look at each other.

Oudry One foot in front of the other. Go and get it done.

Stef I'm not Anne-Marie I'm just doing my job.

Anne-Marie Why tell me but not Tony?

Stef He'd try and stop me.

Anne-Marie And I won't?
Or maybe I would be impressed?

Stef ■
I probably wanted to impress you.

Anne-Marie You really want to impress me: speak honestly. Not in *meeting-mouth* language. Speak honestly to me.

Stef I do, Anne-Marie I really value your

Anne-Marie Bullshit. Speak honestly. You don't tell the committee about your attack. You don't tell us the band has a death threat.

Stef I'm going to sort that.

Anne-Marie And you promise one-third Congolese. But not to listen to us just to look good.

Stef Not for me it's not.

Oudry could begin to sing a note or theme.

Anne-Marie To you I'm just a Congolese for your campaign. But what else am I to you?

Stef I think you're becoming a friend.

Anne-Marie Your friend from a bad place.

Stef That's all you let me see.

Anne-Marie I am lucky. I am safe here. If I don't work for back home, I can never look my community in the face.
Good luck with these men. (*Softly.*) I think you are foolish for going.
Call me, when you are finished, eh. I need your flyers to give at the protest.

Anne-Marie exits. Oudry could halt his song and beam at Stef.

FOURTEEN

DEVILS AND LANTERNS

Maurice's internet cafe. Maurice, William, Nounou.

Maurice <Closing early today, sister.>

Nounou <I paid for an hour, I've had forty-six minutes>

Maurice <The problem with the internet business,
William, is users think they deserve unlimited access.>

Nounou <You don't run Apple, brother, you pour apple
juice.>

Maurice <Whatever, we are closed now, sister.>

Nounou <Is William leaving?>

Maurice <He's staying to work on something.>

William <I'm directing a little movie.>

Nounou <Mm hmm. About?>

■

<Something good and positive I hope.>

William <Always.>

Maurice <One pound for one hour.>

Nounou <Forty-five minutes and you make me leave
early. D'you not see which way the wind is blowing,
brother? The internet is in my phone, soon it's in my
glasses and then in my head. You think then we will need
to come to a café? Especially one that smells like a goat
pen.>

Nounou pays and leaves.

William <Luis won't be pleased.>

Maurice <I said we wouldn't have the numbers. And now with the Parliament woman coming.>

William <I don't think he knows.>

Maurice <I put it in the email>

William <Yeah but he won't've read the email.>

Maurice <I don't write these emails for fun y'know>

William <Yeah, that's really clear actually. What if Luis doesn't want to meet her?>

Maurice <We can't ignore her, this is a woman from *Parliament*.>

William <So fuck Parliament.>

Maurice <Yes obviously fuck Parliament but. *Parliament*. Powerful people pay *us* a visit.>

William <How long before she comes?>

Maurice <She's coming about nine so>

William <I have to direct it in thirty minutes?>

Victor enters.

Maurice <Closed, brother>

Victor <That's early.>

Maurice <Yeah, we closed early.>

Victor <You don't look closed.>

Maurice <Well, this is what closed looks like.>

Victor <I just came to send one bit of money, then I'm gone.>

Maurice <Can't, brother.>

Victor <My mama's waiting for it.>

Maurice <It's Western Union, brother, go to your barbers, newsagent>

Victor <My mama, back in Kin. Will be on the bus at six a.m. Struggled out the house – she's on a stick, I've told you she's on a stick – listens at the gate for bandits because her dog died and she can't replace him. Over the pot-holes and the trash to the stop and waited two three buses>

Maurice <It's like watching a charity appeal>

Victor <Till there's a space and she's on that wooden bench squashed up with twenty people on the bus.>

Maurice <Can I sponsor you to be quiet?>

Victor <And the look on her face, brother, when her man at Western Union says, 'Mama Patricia, there is nothing for you today.' That look belongs to you. The look on her face Maurice, belongs to you.>

☐

Maurice <How much?>

Victor <Brother, you're a great man, can I ask you something?>

Maurice <Quickly.>

Victor <I need help to send her the normal amount.>

Maurice <Don't joke.>

Victor <I have a big payment next week, seriously.>

Maurice <I own a cow in heaven but I can't drink her milk.
  Tell me. Are you busy now, brother?>

Victor <Busy tryin' to help my Mama.>

Maurice <After this?>

Victor <Dinner. Why?>

Maurice <We're making a video.>

Victor <Who's we?>

William <I'm directing.>

Victor <Oh no.>

William <We don't need your face.>

Maurice <We need your feet to step on a picture of the arsehole president.>

William <The arsehole president.>

Maurice <We promised on the blog the video would go up tonight.>

William <But we have very very few brothers available to make it.>

Maurice <I will put your usual amount through in the usual way.>

   □ *Victor nods and hands Maurice cash. Maurice begins processing it.*

Victor <Let me just tell them I will be late.>

   He exits.

Maurice <Don't forget. Parliament-woman is *not* coming to meet the Combattants.>

William <Are we saying we're only the tech people again?>

Maurice <We're the media technology arm of Les Combattants. No knowledge of certain activities.>

   Luis enters with a big bag.

Luis <How are we for time?>

Maurice <Actually, not great.>

Luis <We've got an hour?>

Maurice <We're meeting that woman from Parliament in half an hour.>

Luis <Tonight?>

Maurice <I did put it in the email.>

Luis <This video is meant to be impressive, is meant to be a statement.>

Maurice <If you had read the email>

Luis <No one reads the emails, have you not worked that out yet?>

Maurice <I was getting a sense of it.>

Luis <Have you never heard of bullet points?>

Maurice <I'm not as fond of bullets as you, brother.>

Luis ∎

Maurice <All I'm saying is proper organisations have proper emails.>

Victor enters.

Luis <Closed.>

Maurice <No he's, he's with us.>

Luis <Indeed?>

Victor ∎
<Yes, brother.>

Luis <Welcome, Papa Victor.>

William <As director, I think we should get started.>

Luis <We're waiting for the rest.>

William <This is it.>

Luis <This? I expected low numbers but>

Maurice <Joshua's boys have all gone to Brussels.>

William <Samuel and his guys had to work.>

Maurice <And the Kitenge brothers are on holiday.>

Victor <At home?>

Maurice <The Lake District.>

Victor <You can't call them lakes in this country.>

Maurice <Ponds really>

Victor <The pond district.>

Luis <I have an idea. Right, brothers, trousers off. You too Papa Victor.>

Victor <Eh, what sort of video is this?>

Maurice <It's fine it's fine, we wear these combats>

He opens the large bag. In it are camouflage combat trousers and boots.

Luis <And get me the receipt from the bag. The only way to live in this country is get very clever about tax.>

Victor <You run a printer repair business. How are you gonna claim a bag of camouflage trousers?>

Maurice <How would you know about paying tax, brother?>

Victor ■

Victor starts taking his trousers off. William tugs at Maurice's boxer shorts.

William <I like these, D and G huh?>

Maurice <Leave me alone down there.>

Luis <Trousers are stationed here. We change *here*. Remember which ones you've had on. We only have half an hour because this idiot organised to meet the woman from Parliament.>

Victor <Who?>

Maurice <The woman Cartwright, from the meeting.>

Luis <You know her of course.>

Victor ■
   <I really cannot stay.>

Maurice <Brotherbrotherbrother, bad choice.>

Victor <Why's she coming here?>

William <C'mon I've got to direct this in twenty minutes.>

Maurice <We said we'll listen. About what they're doing for Congo.>

Luis <What they're *not* doing for Congo.>

Victor <I don't uh, I don't want to speak to her.>

Maurice <It might be lies, but we promised.>

Luis <He's embarrassed to be associated with us. Aren't you, Papa Vic?>

Victor <I'm just tired of political talk.>

Maurice <If you have to go, I'll have to double your interest. I'll have to tell Parliament-woman why you only send your money with me, why your business isn't in your name, or your charity which isn't a charity, or your lease, and you have Lebara pay-as-you-go phone and can't even get a contract.>

Luis <She'd be interested.>

   ■

Victor <As long as I go before she arrives.>

Maurice <You have time.>

William <How many times are we going round?>

Luis <We should each go through at least four times.>

William <We did say I was directing it.>

Luis <Whatever, you are, give me a look.>

The framed picture is placed on the floor. A camera on a tripod (or a selfie-stick wedged in something) trained on it.
The four men form a line.

<Action.>

William <Action.>

One by one the men walk slowly over the picture, lingering to stamp on the face.
Once each man is out of shot, he runs behind the camera and puts on a new pair of combat trousers and rejoins the line. After a few turns, the timing is slightly out and Luis has not changed in time. Victor is left stamping up and down on the picture waiting for him.

Victor <Brother, this is ridiculous.>

Luis <Alright alright, cut.>

William <Cut>

Luis <You've got to take longer over it.>

Victor <Are you joking! I was just marching on the spot.>

Luis <Everyone. We've all got to take longer.
Go again. Okay, action.>

William <Action.>

The repeat the procession with better timing. A loud polyphonic ring tone.

Luis <Oh for God's sake! Cut!>

William <Cut!>

Maurice <That's *your* phone, brother Luis.>

William <(*chuckling*) That's not our fault.>

Luis <You're director, aren't you?>

William <Yep.>

Luis <So *remind* everyone to turn their phone off! Basics. Absolute basics.>

Victor <I'm sorry, I really think that's all the time I have tonight.>

William <One more take, Papa Victor.>

Victor <No no, I'm going, sorry.>

Maurice <You've only been here five minutes.>

Luis <You're scared of a woman in a business suit, uh?>

Victor <No, I feel stupid doing this and so should you.>

Luis <You think the future of our country is stupid, brother?>

Victor <Absolutely not.>

Luis <This is just a little YouTube film. It might seem stupid to you. But it's to tell people back home we are not fearful. We are free. To say and do things that at home would have us thrown in gaol. Killed. Tortured. Who are you to laugh at us, expressing our righteous hatred for a man who steals from his people and lets them die?>

Victor <Mobutu stole from us too but / you like him>

Luis <Who are you, mister businessman, who wants to be European. Who wished he could change the colour of his face as well as his passport. If he only had one.>

Victor grabs Luis. There is a protracted scuffle where Victor and Luis can't fight effectively because their trousers are round their ankles.
    Stef enters.

Stef Oh, sorry.

The men attempt to pull their trousers up. Oudry enters.

Luis You should call us first.

Stef I just did.

■

Luis You're early.

Stef I apologise, I was told we didn't have much time.
    Hello, Victor, I didn't uh. I didn't know you were involved with, this.

Victor Well, the diaspora, everybody knows everybody. You know.

Stef And it's you four?

Maurice It is today.

Victor Not me really.

Luis We are the media representatives of Les Combattants de Londres. They have over sixty members and are affiliated to groups in Belgium, France and Germany. We understand you have something to say that we can pass on to them.

Stef Yes. I'm here to say that CongoVoice festival is not their enemy. Our committee is one-third Congolese – as Victor may have

Victor Stephanie, no.

Stef No?

Luis \<Are you with the Parliament, Papa Vic?\>

Victor I think the problems are bigger

Stef Of course and as a committee member

Victor You've made a mistake, I'm not a committee member.
    \<My organisation has sent me to meetings, of course, but I'm not committee\>

Stef Sorry, yes, I made a mistake you're not a committee member.

Victor Really, now I must go.
    \<You won't be disrespectful, brothers\>

William \<Don't forget your trousers, brother.\>

Victor Stephanie.

He leaves.

Luis \<Victor too eh.\>

William \<When are we gonna shoot this film?\>

Stef Gentlemen, you feel strongly about your homeland.

William Natural for Congolais.

Maurice The Congolese diaspora give more money to home than any African diaspora. Western Union figures prove this.

Stef And I don't blame you for being angry. In that spirit I even understand you throwing red Eosin at me. It's not acceptable, but I'm sorry if you felt disrespected.

Maurice (*genuinely confused*) Eosin? When?

Luis We do not recognise this act you speak of.

Stef I haven't reported it yet. I'm not sure that I will. I think we need to find a way to co-exist.

Maurice <Did we throw red at her?>

Luis Co-exist, Miz Cartwright, do you know the old story of the white devil with the lantern?

Stef Can you remind me?

Luis In colonial times, the white man would come to a village at night to round up men, to force them to work. Cutting trees for palm oil, rubber, all these things. Belgian officials would come and take them for this. In the night always, they say, come follow this light. But then the lantern has evil inside. Men never came home. They die from working for the white devil. It's a story for all Congolese.

Stef I see.

Luis That was Europeans trying to co-exist. But now the white man with the lantern, he is outsourcing. You know outsourcing? Now the white man doesn't come to the village. An African comes. But the white man makes the money from the work.
   Before the white man had his lantern, his new technology.
   And still the white man has his new technology.
   And we pay for this, in blood.

Stef It's a very evocative case.

Luis It's a very true case.

Stef But I don't think it's that simple.

Luis Nothing can be simple to the European mind. Everything is taken away. One man Lumumba raise the alarm in 1960, he is killed. Everything is taken, always. And the European mind says oh yah yah yah, it is not simple, wave a hand in the air, nothing is simple. And with the other hand keep taking. Keep take take take.

Stef I sympathise with what you're saying probably more than

Luis But you take from us now with your festival – only you don't know it.

Stef You are taking too. From your culture, you're stopping Congolese music being heard in this country.

Luis My eyes are full of tears.

☐

William Also they are on Spotify.

Stef Y'know what. I heard you might have more influence in the Combattants than this. But if you're just the IT crowd, I'm obviously wasting my time.

Stef turns coolly and begins to walk out.

Maurice No no, Miz Cartwright, you are not wasting your time.

Stef Why don't I give you gents a second to agree how much influence you actually have? Is this the loo?

William nods. Stef leaves to the toilet. Maurice is about to address Luis when he remembers something.

Maurice No! Miz Cartwright, please. Not in there!

Stef walks out choking from the smell.

Sorry sorry! <Everyday with this guy.> That is not from us, we have problem neighbours.

Luis Listen to me, Miz Cartwright. Of course we have influence.

Maurice But not in illegal matters.

Stef So use your influence. Stop the death threats to this band.

Maurice Miz Cartwright, this is always the danger with a political band.

Stef But they're not political.

Maurice They do political concerts for the President.

Stef One public concert, not political, the President just happened to be there.

Luis He was *there*. That is political.

Stef We don't support him. We make no political statements.

Luis You are backed by your Parliament. You are a political statement.

Stef Actually our Parliament insists the campaign is not political at all.

Luis Your Parliament! When Kabila stole the election for the second time, did your Parliament do anything? They help him. They helped because they like him in dere. Your parliament like Kabila. Your Parliament like the money from the technology. People in your Cabinet are on the board of companies who profit from our minerals. Panama Papers tell us that British Virgin Islands pass all the money from our gold. The business interests are too much. Your Parliament now wants to say, oh no, stop. A man is going to read a poem. People will dance. You understand fucking nothing. You invite bands to play, friends of the President. And the Combattants are very angry about this.

So one day, one day soon all the diaspora in Europe will have a great day where they destroy Congolese government, throw out UN, throw out Rwanda, throw out white devils and lanterns.

That day, we will fucking dance and sing.

Now. You can go.

Maurice Papa Luis

Luis No.
  Now she can go.

  ■

Stef Can I tell this band the threat will be dropped?

Luis Go.

Stef I want to tell them that.

Luis Tell them anything. But I expect your festival to be stopped. By force.

Stef So you do make threats.

Luis No. I make predictions.

  ■

Stef Thank you for your time.

Maurice Thank you, Miz Cartwright.

  Stef exits. Oudry leaves with her.

FIFTEEN
WHAT SHE STARTS

The band play and Oudry sings with them.

Oudry (*sings*) Dear Stephanie. Due to security concerns, my clients RumbaNation can no longer play your CongoVoice festival. Death threats from pressure group Les Combattants de Londres have made the trip too great a risk. We wish you fortitude in your endeavour.
  Fortuna Music Management, Paris

  The band finish abruptly and walk off. Oudry remains with microphone.

Kat enters. Oudry is setting up a loop-pedal to his microphone.

Kat Tony Jarman's just coming through security.
I saw that email come in. Looked bad.

Stef There are other bands.

Kat Absolutely.
Stephanie, now's a terrible time but

Stef You need to go home.

Kat No. No I need a reference.

Stef What for? This is a *top* internship.

Kat No, this is full-time! Sustainable Waste campaign.
They asked me to apply!

Stef Wow. Okay.

Oudry uses the loop-pedal to make soundtracks underscoring the scene.

Kat With your reference, I should get it.

Stef Well, you've been wonderful to work with. And I'd never stand in anyone's way, in terms of progressing.

Kat Thank you so much.

Oudry overlays his voice on itself to create a choir.

Stef But I do have a duty of care to safeguard your reputation.

Kat ■
How'd you mean?

Stef Someone could look at your CV and go, two internships, neither completed. Can she finish what she starts?

Kat But you pulled me out of the last internship

Stef We–ll, you probably shouldn't have let me, to be honest.

Kat But this is what I want to do.

Stef I am not going to write you a reference in the next few weeks.

Kat My rent is killing me!

Oudry's choir grows.

Stef Until after the festival, when we both have a clear head.
You'll learn a lot from how you react to this.

Kat ■

Kat leaves. Oudry's choir peaks and dies away.
Tony enters. Oudry begins building a rhythmic beat under the scene.

Tony We have to have a band. We could ask that one I told you about. Indie covers in a rumba style. And they're mostly not Congolese, so threats are less of a problem. Any good for us?

Stef Never thought I'd be happy our band are mostly not Congolese.

Oudry Great house band booked for Hashtag CongoVoice festival: 'Rumba-stious'. Hear Western rock like you've never heard it before. Please RT.

A book fair. Stef and Ira Coleman. Oudry's beat cuts out.

Stef I mean it, you read your work with such elegance and. Precision.

Ira Wow. You must be really stuck for acts huh.

Stef I had no right to question you. The work speaks for itself.

Ira You had the right, same as I had the right to send it back.

Stef Our spot for a reading by the finest writer on the Congo still stands. If you happen to still be free.

Ira My professor at Harvard had a saying: flattery is just an insult in a Sunday coat.

Stef Great line.

Ira Can I ask you a serious question? What the fuck hope of doing anything has your little festival got?

Stef □
The truth is the first festival probably won't be great shakes. I mean, it'll be a hell of a lot better if you're involved. But it *will* be a precedent that will attract twice the funding and we'll triple in size within six months. 'Save Darfur' made a real difference. We aim for that traction within thirty months. If we *don't* get started, that will discourage future attempts and the Congo will stay a nothing issue here.

Ira Send me an email. Suggest what I could read.
And I'll come do my thing, and maybe dance to your band.

Stef Brilliant. Everyone will be delighted.

They part.
Stef on her smartphone. Yawns as she types. Oudry builds another beat.

Oudry Award-winning author Ira Coleman added to CongoVoice bill. Tickets still available, selling fast. Please RT. Hashtag CongoVoice.

A bedroom recording studio.
Stef smiles politely. Ian counts them in silently. A jingle plays from the band.

Ian (*reads*) Hello, you're listening to Aid Matters Podcast sponsored by Blackwell Books, Gower Street. With us now, Stephanie Cartwright, a graduate of the SOAS Conflict and Development Master's and currently co-ordinator of the flagship campaign CongoVoice. It's a role Stephanie secured against some very stiff competition – not least Jenny Walton of Human Rights Monitor who we featured in episode seven.

Stef makes a bit of a face at him.

The campaign and its opening festival currently appear to be in turmoil: acts dropping out, confusion over its constitution, the festival is becoming a lightning rod for diaspora discontent. All in all a case study of a promising campaign going awry. Stephanie – welcome – are you starting to feel you took this role before you were ready?

Stef laughs in practised, professional amusement.

Stef Well, Ian, thank you for having me. And thank you for absolutely roasting me with that first question, but the festival is actually picking up pace in the most exciting way.

Stef puts her hand over the mic.

I'm sorry *what* the fuck are you doing?

Ian stops recording.

Ian Do *not* touch the mic! That mic is the most expensive piece of kit in a ten-mile radius.

Stef Don't stitch me up, Ian.

Ian Have you ever listened to this podcast? I ask the hard questions – that's / my whole thing

Stef I haven't time to listen to my voicemails, Ian, let alone your *hard questions*. You do your intro again, act like a fucking *professional*, not a bedroom wannabe. And don't question the credibility of my event.

Ian I question what I like. That's why I'm independent

Stef Oh, because you *love* being independent do you.

How about if this goes well I will email a BBC World Service producer and tell her two things. One – that she should listen to your podcast. And two – that I'm looking forward to being her bridesmaid this summer.

Now ask me about why my campaign is going to work.

Oudry could up the tempo of the beat. And add to it.

Oudry Dear Sally! Hope wedding prep is not a nightmare. Thank you for the plug for the festival last week. We had a spike in sales! So – I have copied in Ian Wandless, he runs the most fascinating podcast . . .

Victor, Stef and Tony.

Victor I can't tell you why.

Stef You're joking!

Tony It is a bit of a blow, mate.

Victor I can't tell you why but it is not possible

Stef I have no idea what to make of it, Victor. I find you making some ridiculous paramilitary video. You assure me, and Anne-Marie assures me, you're not in the Combattants. But next thing I hear you're leaving the festival and the committee. Do you know how much of a pain in the arse that is, at this point?

Tony Stef

Stef Is it because of the poems? Tell me it's not cos of the fucking poems.

Tony She's tired

Victor It's not the poems.

Stef So it's the boys from the internet café?

Victor I cannot tell you why.

Stef You're like everyone else, you're going to reward the actions of these men playing at soldiers.

Victor I'm sorry – there are other Congolais you can find who don't have my problem.

Stef We don't know what your problem is!

Tony If your problem's a threat of violence, we'll understand

Victor It's not.
I'm sorry. I come today to tell you myself, because I have respect. For you two, for your idea. But

Stef But not the respect to tell us why?

Victor I cannot. Only I am too much living in the light and I must go back and live more in the dark.

Stef Very poetic.

Victor exits. Oudry abruptly stops the pedal.

Stef and Tony, later. Oudry starts the pedal again.

Tony You need to get some sleep

Stef Hundreds of Congolese in this country, we cannot get three to be on a committee.

Tony And stop shouting at people who tried to help us.

Stef Our Steering Committee currently is: you, me, Samo, whose people are giving good money, Jenny fucking bitch face from HRM, who is giving good money.

Tony Yep

Stef No Victor now, one fewer Congolese, but his people were giving almost no money. Anne-Marie, whose money is not make or break. Fred Fletcher, Conflict Minerals and Jeremy McGuire from Street Child, both big donors.

Tony One Congolese, six non-Congolese.

Stef So we need two more Congolese. One more meeting where we sign off the payments – Anne-Marie is being a darling and handing out CongoVoice flyers at a protest tomorrow. A great place to get some more Congolese for the committee. I want to go but. She's a little sick of me at the moment. We've probably seen too much of each other. She likes you.

Tony (*sighs*) Seriously? Flyering.

Stef There's two generations of Congolese you can't reach on social media.

Tony That's not what I meant.

Stef Now I must call Evian and say we're definitely going ahead

Tony Weren't Evian scared off?

Stef No they're sponsoring the shop – books and refreshments.

Tony Evian are like sponsorship cockroaches in a nuclear – hold on

Stef They're loyal

Tony Simon. Simon used to work for Evian.

Stef Simon as in?

Tony Simon your boyfriend after me.

Stef □
Yes he did.

Tony Does he still?

Stef Yes.

Tony And the insane deal you got on web advertising? You got a guy in that port?

Stef I'm not some monster for getting free advertising

Tony It's alright, it's cool, I understand how you work.

Stef Because you've read my emails.

Tony You get things done.

Stef Damn right

Tony You're industrious, you exploit people. That's what industrious people do.

Stef I think you might be making a bit much of this

Tony Is there anyone in your sexual past, or sexual present, that you haven't asked for a favour on this project?

She pretends to think seriously about this.

Stef I had a threesome with two Frenchmen on my gap year.
Haven't asked either of them.

Tony □
Is that. Is that true?

Stef Forgot to get their email.

SIXTEEN
FROM THE KNEES

Anne-Marie and Suzanne outside. It is quiet. There are boxes of flyers. Anne-Marie is perhaps locking up the door to the room they are stored in.
   Suzanne is allowing an upside down placard to lean on her, it reads 'Is Your Mobile Phone Helping Fund War in Congo?'

Anne-Marie stops and looks at her bored daughter.

Anne-Marie Look, I am not stupid. I know this does not interest you. When Tony is back you can go home.

Suzanne Don't make out like you're doing me a favour, you want me home so someone's with Grandpapa.

Anne-Marie I am not Estelle from school, young lady. You can speak to me / with respect.

Suzanne He calls me your name all the time, he doesn't even know who is looking after him.

Anne-Marie Papa has moments of confusion, but he is more sick in his body than his mind.

Suzanne But – how would you know though? You're not there. It's worse than you think.

Anne-Marie Hold these for me.

Tony enters and is about to pick up a box to carry.

Tony Right, I can start lugging them up I think.

Anne-Marie Do we need this many?

Tony I want to take the rest of them off in an uber after the protest.
Right, load me up.

Anne-Marie loads him up with a box.

Yep and again.

Anne-Marie bends for another.

From the knees.
So you happy with the design?

Anne-Marie I think the Parliament logo could be smaller you know. For the Congolais.

Tony I think it had to be that size. Yep and another.

Anne-Marie Sure?

Tony No, I can take more than that.

It becomes a bit of a game, loading him up. Anne-Marie giggles. Suzanne does not see her mum like this very often.

Anne-Marie You will drop all this.

Tony Go on, tuck one in. This is what I go to the gym for.

Anne-Marie You go to the gym?

Tony Well. I have done.

Anne-Marie giggles. Suzanne is mortified at their flirting.

Suzanne So I never thought I'd say this but. I really wanna get home to look after my Grandpapa.

Suzanne plants a perfunctory kiss on Anne-Marie and leaves.

Anne-Marie jokingly tries to balance one too many boxes on Tony.

Tony Actually this is loads. Stick a couple of boxes away and I'll come back and help with the rest.

Anne-Marie has some loose flyers.

Anne-Marie (*playing*) I know.

She stuffs the loose flyers in his pocket. He is about to leave.

Wait.

She stuffs some loose flyers in his other pocket.

For balance.

Tony smiles at her warmly.

Tony Good job.

He starts lugging the flyers away.

Anne-Marie is beginning to put the spare boxes back.

A man with his face hidden enters stealthily. He has been watching.

Perhaps this act is accompanied by a lone, slow drum.

He comes behind Anne-Marie. He puts his hand over her mouth and an arm around her neck.

Anne-Marie struggles.

Another man enters similarly dressed.

He stands, still looking down at her.

He casually takes a flyer and looks at it. Then scrumples it up.

The drumbeat could become more insistent.

The second man pulls out a revolver and holds it in front of her face.

The hand is taken from her mouth and she makes a half-scream before the flyer is forced into her mouth and closed around it. They try to make her chew it. She lets out a cry of panic.

The second man puts the revolver to her eye. He pulls it away and with his other hand he punches her hard in the same eye.

The band could start playing fully.

Tony runs back in.

The second man winds back once more and smacks her directly in the eye.

Tony is sent flying by one of the men as they suddenly sprint away.

When Tony is knocked over maybe the flyers in his pockets go everywhere.

Anne Marie lies in agony clutching her eye. Tony crouches over her.

Suzanne runs in, sees her mother and screams, rooted to the spot.

SEVENTEEN
THE BETTER PART

Portcullis House. Stef with Huw and Jenny.

Huw I just spoke with her.

Jenny Is it true she may lose the sight in one eye?

Stef Moorfields are very positive. She has another retinal scan in a couple of days. And she's in good spirits, back home and walking around.

Jenny With police protection now at least.

■

Stef Come on then.

Huw There's no easy way of saying this.

■

Stef Why, what is it, a Welsh village?

Huw In light of what's happened, it might be wise, as far as this year is concerned, to say that discretion is the better part of valour.

Stef And call it off.

Huw And call it off, yes. The attack gives us a chance to call it off and regroup, without admitting defeat.

Stef Calling it off is defeat

Huw Defeat is any more people hurt, any more acts dropped out, any more embarrassment than we've already had.

Stef And this is a decision you and Jenny have come to together?

Jenny There's no decision

Huw It's just a conversation.

Stef That you had without me.

Huw That we're having now.

■

Stef Well then, thank you, I'll take it all on board.

She goes to leave.

Huw Stephanie. If you're not willing to act, I'm afraid I may have to pull rank.

Stef And I'm afraid, I don't think you can.

Huw Sorry?

Stef I'm afraid, you're not my boss, you're the MP for Clwyd West. Sure you can get a vote of no confidence, but you have ten days and you'd have to cause a big fuss. It was your call to appoint me, it's egg on your face. And I won't go quietly.

Huw All this, hardly worth destroying a career, and a friendship, over. Is it?

Stef ■

Huw One small festival?

Jenny At the moment it's not even that.

Stef It may be underwhelming this year but we will / build

Jenny We don't have one-third Congolese support.

Stef We will have.

Jenny How?

Stef By the final steering meeting when we sign off on things

Jenny Which is tomorrow

Stef We will have one-third Congolese.

Jenny At the moment there are none.

Stef Anne-Marie.

Jenny Nope.

Stef If you think Anne-Marie being attacked has put her off, it's made her twice as determined.

Huw Her father has just died.

Stef Oh

Huw So I think that's it as far as her involvement goes.

Stef Did she say that?

Jenny Look

Stef Did she say that?

Huw She said that, yes.

■

I'm sorry. Let's try again next year. It's not like Congo's gonna be fixed by then is it? We need to tell people by tomorrow morning.

He exits.

Jenny For what it's worth, Human Rights Monitor would still be willing to support it.

Stef If I step down.

Jenny No. I've discussed it with others on the committee and we'll allow you to change the constitution.

Stef Who else?

Jenny Samo. Jeremy from StreetChild.

Stef Jeremy from Streetchild of course

Jenny Jeremy's playing an active part, he's just been unable / to make

Stef Aren't you and Jeremy playing an *active part*? At the moment?

Jenny That's a shame, I thought you were better than that.

Stef Just the rumour mill?

Jenny Jeremy has his own mind.
    We are prepared to forgo this constitutional necessity of one-third Congolese support. We think it'll be a better campaign.

Stef That constitution. Is everything.

Jenny You'll be surprised how little you miss it.

Stef CongoVoice without a Congolese voice

Jenny Just because they're Congolese doesn't mean they're the right people to run a campaign. All they have is their guilt that they got out. And a need to exercise it in public. I've worked with lots of diasporas, it's not specific to Congo. And you fell for it. You've ruined a whole festival, to involve people who don't want to be involved.

Stef We will have enough Congolese. By tomorrow's meeting.
    The constitution stays.

Jenny (*goes to leave, stops.*) Stephanie. You were in South Kivu about a year ago, weren't you?

Stef Yes.

Jenny Observing the International Medical Corps?

Stef I was. Why?

Jenny What did you think of the work they were doing?

Stef Exceptional. They saved hundreds of lives.

Jenny I secured the funding for that project.

Stef Oh. I didn't know that.

Jenny There was a nurse you met. A Canadian. I had to fill out an assessment of whether you were put at undue risk.

Stef ■
What did you decide?

Jenny I can't remember. I had a lot of other things to do.

Jenny leaves.

Stef's office. Later. Tony and Stef. Oudry with them.

Stef Jenny has positioned herself perfectly, for when, if. This all goes

Tony To shit.

Stef Yeah. She has positioned herself perfectly for that.

Tony has found a carton of UmBongo with a little note on it. He hands it to Stef.

(*Reads.*) 'You probably shouldn't have let me.' Kat's left. Didn't know they still made it.
(*Sucks through the straw.*) God, it's good isn't it?
We totally should have got this whole thing sponsored by them.

Tony I think they're probably quite limited in terms of / financial

Stef I'm joking, Tony. CongoVoice Festival sponsored by fucking UmBongo tropical juice drink. I'm not completely insane.
How you doing?

Tony Still a bit shaken.

Stef Course you are, anyone would be.

Tony It would've been different if my mum had let me do karate.

Stef Sure.

Oudry Don't look at the man.

Stef What are you doing tonight? Come over to Anne-Marie's place

Tony Is she scared to come out?

Stef No, her dad's died.

Tony Oh. Shit.
  I s'pose he'd been ill for ages but

Stef She's dropped out of the festival.

Tony Woawoawoah. Are we going to persuade her not to leave the festival when her dad's just died?

Oudry One foot in front of the other.

Stef We're going to pay our respects.

Tony And she's just been attacked

Stef It's a wake.

Tony A wake?

Oudry Go and get it done.

Stef Yeah, a wake.
  Lots of Congolese people.

Tony Oh no.

Stef We need three people

Tony They're grieving. It's not a recruitment mission

Oudry Don't look at the wound.

Stef Three people of demonstrable Congolese descent, to come to a meeting tomorrow. And put their hand up.

Tony It's not appropriate.

Stef It's one of the most beautiful things you've ever heard, everyone goes straight round to the house of the deceased and sits with the family. And eats. And drinks and talks. For days. To support.

Tony Do we need to wear black?

Stef I looked it up. No.

EIGHTEEN
THE WAKE

Anne-Marie's flat. Evening.
A lounge area. A hallway off it with a front door and a landing outside it.
In the lounge. Victor and Suzanne. Nounou finishes setting a table cloth, then leaves. Suzanne is staring at the floor.

Victor I found my father, you know. Years ago, in Congo.
Big big heart attack. His body twisted all around. Like an old tree. But also I felt, for myself, I am happy it was me.
I am happy that it was me that find my father. Maybe you can be happy you found your grandfather.

Anne-Marie has entered with a large patch over her eye. She carries cutlery.

<Sister, can I help with anything?>

Anne-Marie <No, Victor, thank you, Nounou is here. Eat.>

Suzanne Mum?

Anne-Marie Yes?

Suzanne Nothing.

Anne-Marie leaves the lounge.
In the hallway Nounou catches Anne-Marie.

Nounou <Eh, you know they're gonna come.>

Anne-Marie <Of course>

Nounou <You don't have to let them.>

Anne-Marie <Today, I do.>

Nounou <Papa Albert wouldn't want men who beat you in his house.>

Anne-Marie <We don't know it was them.>

Nounou <This doesn't make it easier! Pretending you don't know.>

Anne-Marie <I'm pretending nothing. Probably it was them. But I don't know.
   They won't do anything today.>

Nounou <No, not today but they shouldn't be welcome.
   I'm gonna text now and say don't come. They wouldn't argue on the day your Papa dies. Yeah?>

Anne-Marie ■
   <Let them pay their respects.>

Nounou <They need to pay you respect.
   But it's your call.
   Did Albert leave anything?>

Anne-Marie <Oh, no. But I knew that.>

Nounou <Eh, is your Kevin Costner here?>

Anne-Marie <Stop it.>

   She exits into the kitchen.
   In the lounge. A DVD of Congolese music. Victor and Suzanne.

Victor How is your mother with her injuries?

Suzanne Dunno, arx her.

Victor And she has police security?

Suzanne Outside. In a car. There's two, one for the day, one for the night.

Victor looks out of a window. Anne-Marie and Nounou enter from the kitchen with trays of traditional Congolese food – pondu, cassava etc.

Nounou Suzanne you are looking more beauteous every day. You're going to be a beautiful African woman.

Victor <How are your injuries, sister?>

Anne-Marie <Compared with the women at home, nothing.>

Victor <This must be a big shock today.>

Anne-Marie <Do you think.>

Victor <Death doesn't sound a trumpet.>

Nounou <Death doesn't sound a trumpet indeed.>

Anne-Marie <When a man is ill for two years, it sounds a damn trumpet.>

She leaves.

Nounou <I never know what to say either.>
Maybe it can help her come to God.

Nounou follows Anne-Marie out. In the hallway:

Anne-Marie <Why is he the first one here?>

Nounou <Have you talked to your daughter properly?>

Anne-Marie <Did Victor really know my father so well that he is first here?>

Nounou <Have you talked to Suzanne?>

Anne-Marie <Tell me where the time is for that? I've called cousins, nephews, neighbours today. Kinshasa, Brussels, London. I have you interrogating me, my eye hurts, we don't have enough plates, there are people on the way who probably don't think I'm even having a wake because I lost my culture or whatever. Work at eight. Twenty emails from Kivu to translate by Friday.>

Nounou <She's lost her grandpapa.>

Anne-Marie <I live with her, we will get time / to talk.>

Nounou <It's her first death. And she *found* him.>

Anne-Marie ■
<I know, I. You're right. It's strange between us I dunno what I'm thinking.>

Nounou <I'll get some plates from mine.>

Nounou follows Anne-Marie off into the kitchen.
In the lounge:

Victor You like this? The music Congolais?

Suzanne It's 'kay.

Victor Only okay. What music do you like?

Suzanne You won't know it.

Victor Try me. You might be surprised what I know about music.

Suzanne ■

Victor I won't know it will I.

In the corridor. Nounou opens the door to leave and sees Kevin, a black British Policeman (Brummie, Scouse?) Nounou closes the door.

Nounou <Eh, your fancy man is here!>

Anne-Marie emerges from the kitchen.

<Oh apron off, uh? Like that is it?>

Anne-Marie <No, I'm just. Finished.>

> *Nounou starts doing Anne-Marie's hair, Anne-Marie is fighting her off.*

<No, ahhh. I want the hair over the patch.>

> *Kevin's knocking. They're both laughing now.*

<Go and get the plates, you stupid boot, you're like my mama!>

Nounou <And you're like Whitney Houston.> *The Bodyguard.*

> *Nounou opens the door to a bemused Kevin.*

Hello!

Kevin Is Anne-Ma— (*Sees her.*) Hey, is your phone working?

Anne-Marie Sorry.

Nounou Hi, I'm Nounou.

Kevin Hi, I'm Kevin.

Nounou <He's actually called Kevin!>

Kevin You weren't answering your phone.

Anne-Marie Sorry.

Nounou <Don't tell me his surname, this is too perfect>

> *Nounou fails to suppress a laugh. Anne-Marie just about succeeds.*

Kevin Am I doing something funny?

Anne-Marie No, forgive us, it's a strange day.

Nounou <How do I get one of these?>

Anne-Marie <You have to be attacked.>

Kevin When we're handing over outside

Nounou <Is it worth it?>

Anne-Marie <Depends on the man.> Go and get plates!

Nounou I'm going to get plates.

Anne-Marie Yes go, idiot woman.

Nounou leaves, amused. Anne-Marie shakes her head.

Sorry, she is a little crazy.

Kevin You need to be available on the phone when Jerry and me hand over outside. You entertaining guests?

Anne-Marie Kevin, today my father has died.

Kevin Oh. God I'm.

Anne-Marie So this is his wake we start now.

Kevin Oh God, I'm so sorry, Anne-Marie. How are you bearing up?
   You seem in good spirits, you and that lady

Anne-Marie Adrenalin. Little shock maybe. Come in, you are hungry?

Kevin I've got a, a thing in the car.

Anne-Marie A thing?

Kevin A buffet bar.

Anne-Marie You have a *buffet* in your car?

Kevin No it's a. Ginsters buffet *bar*, it's like, I s'pose, some things you *might* have in a buffet, except it's in a bar, that's made of. Meat.

Anne-Marie Come in and have some / real food.

136

Kevin Maybe I'll come in and have some real food. No listen. I can't.

Anne-Marie I have invited you.

Kevin I'm sorry for your loss but, I'm at work and you're still under threat.

Anne-Marie Also there is something to tell you.

Kevin Yeah?

Anne-Marie The suspects. From the attack?

Kevin Yeah?

Anne-Marie They are coming here.

Kevin How do you know! When?

Anne-Marie Well because

Kevin Are you sure?

Anne-Marie Yes I am sure.

Kevin If you're sure, I'm going to call *now* for more security

Anne-Marie No no, wait. I have invite them.

Kevin □
You invited them.

Anne-Marie Well, not exactly but – it's my papa's wake. So they will come.

Kevin Let me get this straight, right, I have one job here, to stop men attacking you. And some of the men we think *might* have attacked you, are coming round for a party.

Anne-Marie It sounds worse like that.

Kevin Aw bloody hell, Anne-Marie.

Anne-Marie I know it's not perfect for you

Kevin Not perfect? You realise I *have* to stop them.

Anne-Marie Please. Kevin, please. It's my papa's wake.
They were at his same church. Please leave them.

Kevin ■
This is madness.

Anne-Marie I beg you. It's very important we not have
a problem at the wake. I promise you they will be fine.

Kevin I have to come in and watch them.

Anne-Marie This is what I said, come in and have food.

Kevin Seriously, this is enough to get me suspended.
Alright, give me one minute.

*He exits. Anne-Marie goes back into the lounge with
Victor and Suzanne.*

Victor Ah, sister. I was just saying, from now on, I could
be round to check on Suzanne. And you. Now you're just
two women here.

Suzanne I don't need checking.

Anne-Marie <Thank you, brother but we're okay.>

Victor Or maybe on a free day, take Suzanne and you to
a theme park?

Suzanne looks at him in disbelief.

Not Alton Towers obviously. Seen enough amputees for
one lifetime!
<I've misjudged this, haven't I?>

Anne-Marie <Brother, we know you mean well.>

She leaves the room.
*More Congolese guests arrive, console Anne-Marie,
take a plate of food.*

Kevin returns. He eats and sizes up newcomers.
Stef and Tony are arriving as Nounou returns with
plates.

Stef Nounou!

Nounou Oh.

Stef Yeah, we heard about Albert.

Nounou You knew Papa Albert?

Stef And we're worried about Anne-Marie, after the
attack.

Tony Hi.

Nounou I'm sorry for your festival.

Oudry slides into the scene.

Stef It's not quite buried yet.

Tony How is Anne-Marie taking it?

Stef We just need a few more Congolese on the steering
committee.

Tony Is she very upset?

Nounou What do you call a person does not feel emotion?

Tony Like. A psychopath?

Nounou Who has no pain?

Stef Numb.

Tony Oh numb, yeah

Nounou She is numb, but come and see her.

Nounou opens the door and they go in. Anne-Marie
sees Stef and Tony.

Anne-Marie (*surprised*) Ah.

Tony We heard.

Stef I'm so sorry about your dad.

She hugs Anne-Marie.
  Nounou takes the plates through to the kitchen.

Anne-Marie Thank you.

Tony Very sorry.

Anne-Marie He is better where he is now.

Stef How is the eye?

Anne-Marie Another scan next week.

Tony You're looking great considering.

Anne-Marie You know, truly I am sorry about your
festival.

Tony This isn't about the festival

Stef It's not about the festival.

Anne-Marie Well, whatever it is, you are welcome.
  There's, uh. There is one thing you should know.
  Ah, go, please eat. You will know some people who
come probably.

Tony I wanted to say, I'm so sorry I couldn't do more.
  When you were attacked.

Anne-Marie Please, don't apologise.

Tony It would've been different if my mum had let me
do karate.

Anne-Marie laughs warmly and leaves to the kitchen.
  *Stef and Tony enter the lounge. Everyone looks at
them.*
  *Victor greets them, serves them food/beer. Nounou
is talking in a group.*

Nounou Look at this wake, this is normal for us. That is the problem, we are too hospitable. Congo is a hospitable country. As a country we pay for our own hospitality. Everyone comes there and take what they want.

In the hallway. Suzanne approaches Anne-Marie.

Suzanne Mum, can I talk to you?

Anne-Marie Of course. (*Holds her arms out.*) Come here.

Suzanne Can I go out?

Anne-Marie What?

Suzanne Can I go to Estelle's house?

Anne-Marie It's your grandpapa's wake!

Suzanne No one's gonna talk to me in English, I might as well not be here

Anne-Marie Am I just a terrible mother?

Suzanne (*sighs*) No.

Anne-Marie Did I raise you so wrong?

Suzanne Fine I'll stay, just don't expect me to talk to anyone.

She walks away. Anne-Marie storms into the kitchen. In the lounge: Stef and Nounou.

Stef My father was, father was the big one for me.

Nounou When you lose your father?

Stef I was twenty-seven. Hit me so hard. Basically quit my job.

Nounou He was a powerful man?

Stef Uh, I suppose he was.

Nounou I can see this actually. What was his job?

Stef Businessman, farmer, hard to say

Nounou Farmer? Where?

Stef Uh, Kenya.

Nounou ■

Nounou nods in comprehension.

Stef You know, all we actually need is for you to come along and vote on one day. Tomorrow.

Nounou This is my community you ask me to be against. My church.

Stef Look at what they did to Anne-Marie. We can't tell them those tactics work.

Nounou No, they know already it work.
Let me think.

Nounou goes for food. Stef surreptitiously looks at her smartphone.

Oudry 'Why Men Pull Away.'
Here are ten reasons why men pull away from women

Stef (*annoyed*) Delete.

Stef catches Tony's eye and indicates Suzanne. Tony shakes his head.
Stef shrugs at him ('Worth a try?'). Tony shakes and mimes her height ('She's a child'). Stef approaches Suzanne anyway.

Hello again. I'm so sorry about your grandfather. It's really hard.

Suzanne He was old, he was always gonna die.

Stef Did you ever visit where he came from?

Suzanne Nope.

Stef So you've never been to Congo?

Suzanne Mum doesn't take me cos of school and. It's not safe or whatever. But I reckon she enjoys it more on her own.

Stef I'm sure it's not that. So you're not dual nationality?

Suzanne Dunno.

Stef Do you have a Congolese passport?

Suzanne Just British. Why?

Stef It's interesting, isn't it. I was born in Kenya, but I don't have a Kenyan passport.

Suzanne ■

Stef My thoughts are with you. Your mum's a brilliant woman.

Stef gets up. Grimaces at Tony. Indicates for him to talk to Kevin.

Tony Can I talk to you about a Congolese festival?

Kevin I'd rather you didn't, mate, to be honest.

Tony Okay. Are you, are you Congolese?

Kevin No, mate, I'm just at work.

Tony Oh, you're the copper?

Kevin nods. Tony taps the side of his nose: 'Your secret's safe.'
Tony returns to Stef and shakes his head.

Stef. Why didn't you invite me to your dad's funeral? We got on.

Stef Quiet affair. Everyone was angry we didn't observe his burial wish.

143

Tony Are you angry with those Kenyans for saying he couldn't be buried there?

Stef No. Because they didn't.

That's just what I told my family. I decided. He didn't belong there.

Outside the flat. Maurice is about to knock. Luis pulls him back.

Luis <Just listen one minute>

Maurice <I am saying farewell to Papa Albert, I am saying sorry for their loss, and I'm going.>

Luis <We will look ashamed.>

Maurice <Well maybe we sh—>

Luis <Maybe we what, brother?>

Maurice <What you do is up to you.>

Luis <It is and what I will not do is look ashamed. I'm glad I never had you by my side in '97, when the streets filled with insects. Because I'd've been a corpse in a gutter.>

Maurice knocks. Nounou opens the door.

Nounou ■

Maurice <Sister>

Nounou <Come to pay respect?>

Maurice <Certainly.>

Nounou <Do you know how to respect?>

Luis <Please. Today is not for bitterness.>

Nounou 'Blessed is he who perseveres under trial.'

Luis Indeed.

Nounou I hope it goes to trial.

They enter the lounge. Anne-Marie nods to Kevin that these are the men.

Anne-Marie <Thank you for coming to my father's wake.>

Maurice <God be with you in your time of loss.>

Anne-Marie <You'll eat with us?>

Maurice <Thank you, but I won't stop.>

Luis <I would love some food.>

He helps himself to food.

Maurice <Also, I was sorry to hear of your>

Anne-Marie <Of my?>

Maurice <Someone obviously went too far.>

Luis <This is what happens when Congolese become involved in traitorous ceremonies.>

Maurice and Luis exchange an angry look.

Nounou <Well, she's not involved now.>

Luis <A brave choice. So many temptations to lead astray the real Congolese.>

Maurice <You have my thoughts, sister, I may be back tomorrow.
Brother Luis.>

Luis <Important emails to write.>

Maurice leaves the flat.

<Sister, I see you have your Parliament friends here.>

Luis nods cordially to Stef, who nods back, steely.

<Let's ask them how we run a Congolese wake. They know so much of our culture. And I hear they're looking for something to do now.>

145

Nounou stares at Luis. And walks away to find Stef.

Nounou I will come tomorrow.

Stef Brilliant!

Stef gestures to Tony: 'One.' Luis approaches Stef.

Luis Miz Cartwright. I'm very sorry to hear of your trouble.

Stef We've had quite a lot of trouble, you'll have to be specific.

Luis Your festival is not to happen.

Stef Where did you hear that?

Luis Everybody knows. Not enough Congolese for your Congolese festival.

Stef Sorry to disappoint you, the festival is going ahead.

Luis Is that so?

Stef It is.

Luis Very good, like brother Malcolm X. (*Laughs.*) 'Any means necessary.'

Tony Hi. Tony Jarman, we met when we had you ejected from the press launch.

Luis Miz Cartwright, you look well today, your complexion, you use a special product for this?

Luis addresses the room.

<Brothers and sisters.> Sorry to interrupt. I am only here for a short time so I would like to speak to everyone.

<We are here to pay our respects to Papa Albert, a Congolese man who never lost his culture. When Papa Albert came here the community was ve–ry small, he was number thirty-eight of the Congolese in London. As he always liked to tell us.>

Some warm laughter.

<He had a great faith and was proud of his family. And he was proud of being Congolais, and would never do anything to hurt Congo or betray it. And in his illness he was brave too.>

Anne-Marie Thanks for your words / brother.

Luis <I hope his family can, honour him. With their conduct. And that Papa Albert's memory is not betrayed.>

Victor <Brother, what do you mean exactly?>

Luis <I honour Papa Albert.>

Victor <No, you insult Mama Anne-Marie in her own home / at her father's wake.>

Anne-Marie There's no problem.

Luis <You're excited, Vic.>

Nounou <Lower your voices!>

Victor <You should apologise to Anne-Marie.>

Anne-Marie <I don't need an apology>

Luis This man Victor is true Congolese. So Congolese, he doesn't even have the British passport. He is illegal! I pay my British taxes. I am proud to do it, they took me when our country was stolen. Do your Parliament friends know how you live in London? About your tax?

Stef It's none of our business.

Anne-Marie <That's why you don't visit your mama.>

Victor Apologise to Mama, Anne-Marie.

Anne-Marie <I'd be ashamed to give a man away like this.>

Luis <I would be ashamed to support an insect president.>

147

Kevin Right I don't understand a word of this but back off.

Victor Apologise!

Luis <I'd be ashamed to work with British Parliament.>

Anne-Marie Stephanie? When is your meeting?

Stef Tomorrow.

Anne-Marie I see you there.

Nounou starts clapping, Stef and Tony join in. Oudry plays his thumb-piano?

Luis <Your father would be fucking ashamed of the godless traitor he brought into this world.>

Victor swings at Luis, misses and Luis hits him to the ground.

Kevin Police! Don't move! You are under arrest for assault, endangering the safety of those around you. Turn around and present your arms behind your back. Now!

With calm dignity, Luis allows himself to be arrested. Kevin takes Luis away.
The scene disperses leaving Suzanne and Anne-Marie alone in the lounge. Later . . . ?

Suzanne <Mum, are you alright?>

Anne-Marie <Say that again.>

Suzanne <Are you alright, do you feel sad?

Anne-Marie <How are you speaking Lingala to me?>

Suzanne I know a bit, Jeez I'm not deaf.

Anne-Marie How you mean, not deaf?

Suzanne <Grandpapa Lingala talk every day.>

Anne-Marie <You don't speak it to me.>

Suzanne <You are never here.>

Anne-Marie <I'm going to be here. I'm quitting all this. I'm going to be here.>

She wraps her daughter up in her arms.

But I must go tomorrow. Last time.

NINETEEN
THE WORST THING

Stef stands alone tapping on her tablet. As the meeting is built around her.

Oudry Dear Congolese friends. Excuse the group email – this is a plea to any of you to attend tomorrow's meeting. Or CongoVoice festival will not go ahead. I urge you to back this imperfect event, this imperfect attempt.
Thank you, Stephanie Cartwright

In the meeting room, Fred, Jenny, Stef and Samo are all waiting, fiddling with smartphones or tablets. People look around awkwardly.

☐

■

Tony enters.

Tony Sorry, not started have we?

Fred Nope, we're waiting for three Congolese people to make anything we say matter.

Jenny I'm afraid it might be more complicated than that. I believe Jeremy has emailed you.

Stef Today? My email's been on the blink.

□ *Stef starts checking her smartphone but thinks better of it.*

Look, let's do what we can without the full committee here. We have some brilliant news: the festival has sold out

Fred Well, I could've told you that.

Stef Yes, the tickets have sold out, Fred. There was a surge after the actor Harry Jandrell tweeted.
 Now circumstances permitting we need to vote to sign off on all the costs and pay them tonight.

Jenny Shouldn't we first talk about what Jeremy from Streetchild has said?

Fred StreetChild's money is still twenty per cent of our budget.

Stef Jeremy hasn't turned up, we can spend his money for him.

Jenny Pains me to say, but it's not the worst thing in the world this festival being called off.

Stef No, the worst thing in the world is what the festival's about.

Jenny Do check your emails, Stephanie.

 Stef goes to check her mails.

Stef 'Deep Tissue Massage 54% off.'
 'Viagra best price in market.'

 Nounou enters. She is welcomed by the room.
  Followed by Anne-Marie in an elegant eye-patch.
 The room rises to her.

Fred Very brave, I hope it's not been in vain.

Samo We are close, but still need

Anne-Marie Another Congolese, yes.

Stef (*to Anne-Marie*) Did anyone get back to you?

Anne-Marie Sorry.

    Stef has accessed her emails.

Oudry 'Amount won 5 million dollars!'
'CongoVoice withdrawal.'
'Prime land can be yours.'

Stef Back.

Oudry 'CongoVoice Withdrawal. Jeremy, Streetchild.'

Stef Open.

Oudry (*sings in an increasingly disturbed way*) In disappointment at the festival's lack of concern for Kinshasa street children. Its unwillingness to consult. We will be pulling all of our funds from CongoVoice Festival and campaign with immediate effect.

Stef ☐
Guys?
It looks like it's over.

    Reaction. General disappointment.
      Victor enters.

Victor This looks the place.

Stef Victor!

Nounou Maybe not finished yet!

Tony Yes!

Fred Oh good for you

Anne-Marie Brother, do you mean this?

Victor Those men don't decide what we do.

Tony You bloody hero, Victor.

Nounou <Brother, what about your situation?>

Anne-Marie <All it takes, one phone call from Luis.>

Victor <If I go home, well. It's in God's hands.>

Nounou <Are you sure, brother?>

Victor <Haven't seen my mama for years.>

Anne-Marie <Even just your name on the committee could be>

Victor <Mama wants me to find a wife. And maybe I cannot here.>

> *Anne-Marie and Victor look at each other. Anne-Marie looks away.*

But I will be here for the festival.

Anne-Marie So it's not over

Jenny I'm afraid it is. I was copied in to an email I think Stephanie's just got.

Stef First you've heard of it, I'm sure

Jenny The festival is thousands of pounds shy. It's very regrettable.

> *Disappointed general reaction.*

Victor You said just come and I have come!

Anne-Marie Always. The same.

Oudry Don't look at the wound.

> *Stef is looking at her smartphone.*

Stef Hold on.

Oudry 'Naturally Low Blood Pressure.'

Stef No, there's a new donor.

Samo Money is through organisations, not donors.

Stef Giving his money to Anne-Marie's organisation

Oudry 'You Deserve a Walk-In Bathtub.'

Stef Who specifies it must go to this project.

Anne-Marie First time I know of this.

Stef It's literally just come in.

Jenny From where?

Stef A good source

Oudry 'Fat loss mega fat loss fat loss miracles.'

Jenny This is irregular in the extreme.

Fred It's got to be done right, Stephanie.

Samo And the money is needed tonight.

Oudry 'Free Pass to All Local Pussies!'

Stef Yes, it can be transferred tonight

Jenny Well, I hope your donor has another twenty thousand pounds.
    Because we're out too.

Stef □
    He. He does. He can cover it.

Tony What's actually happening here?

Anne-Marie Who is this donor? Giving to my organisation?

Stef looks at her phone.

Stef It's an anonymous donor.

Jenny No no no

Fred We can't allow them, you know that

Stef It's through Anne-Marie's women's group.

Jenny Even so, big donors need clearance

Samo We don't allow anonymous

Fred How do we know they're clean?

Stef It's legit, I just can't tell you who it is.

Fred You have to.

Tony No, you don't need to say any more

Samo She does! Do not tell us our job, sir

Tony You don't need to say anything, Stef, just

Jenny Name them.

Samo We have strict rules, they must be checked out.

Tony Let's stop all this now

He gently takes Stef's phone from her hands. Oudry moves outside the scene.

Stef I need that!

Fred Who are they?

Stef We'll have it in cash tonight – Anne-Marie you'll come get it with me?

Anne-Marie From who?

Jenny Absurd.

Fred Really you must

Tony Stef, let's just drop it now

Anne-Marie Tell us, Stephanie, who it is.

Stef It's my father.

∎

Jenny Oh for

154

Samo Your father

Tony Stef, don't say any more.

Stef There's enough to cover the forty thousand pound shortfall.

Samo Did you not say he

Stef He would have wanted this.

Fred and Samo begin to pack up, embarrassed.

Victor <I am seriously confused.>

Nounou <Her father from Kenya.>

Stef I'll get it out in cash!

Tony Stef, please

Stef Tony, shut the fuck up and let me do this – Anne-Marie, will you come and process it?

Anne-Marie Why me?

Stef Because your organisation doesn't have strict rules like they do.

Jenny (*leaving*) Excuse me, ladies and gentlemen.

Anne-Marie We cannot take your guilt money any more than the others.

Stef You can. He fucking made the money in Africa. Let's give it back.

Victor Stephanie, none of us can process that donation

Stef Listen to me, okay – there are ways. This is something I know best about. There's nothing stopping you taking this money.

Anne-Marie Okay.
I will accept the money.

Stef Brilliant! (*Shouting at the door.*) Jenny, it's going through with or without you. Tony get everyone back, we need to vote.

Anne-Marie But if that money is in my organisation. It becomes my responsibility. And I would not spend it on your festival. I would send it to our women's refuge in Goma – it would be gone tomorrow

Stef No, you said you supported this, supported me / you said.

Anne-Marie I support you but forty thousand pounds for dancing and poems, when women lie wounded and dying

Stef And *only* when people give a shit will anything happen, Anne-Marie – that's political will. And *obviously* this festival is bullshit! I mean fucking *obviously*, you think I don't know that? But *when* it goes ahead, more things follow – more funding, more partners, more coverage and we *build*, we build like Chinese fucking industrialists, so that nobody dares mention UmBongo again when they hear that country's name – they mention resilience and brutality, and Leopold and PlayStations, and moral debt and I'm fucking sorry Anne-Marie, just let me put that money through

Anne-Marie I will let you put it through but I will spend it how I like.

Stef But it's *my* money.

Nounou Either it is your money or it's not.

Anne-Marie Once the money is ours, I cannot in good conscience spend it that way. My board will not allow it.

Stef You send it to Congo through your channels – how much gets skimmed off in bribes?

Anne-Marie You don't trust Congolese. Of course. We cannot help ourselves.

Stef How much goes to police, militia, businessmen, officials. You'd be lucky if ten grand made it.

Anne-Marie My channels are corrupt! And your channels are so clean! British tax havens, multinationals, Parliament building paid for / by empire.

Stef Guns, Anne-Marie, that's what you'd be buying, more guns for Congo

Anne-Marie Guns made where? No guns made in Congo. Who holds the most arms fairs in the world? I think you can guess.

Stef Victor, you can process it!

Victor No. My organisation is not in my name. I don't exist here.

Stef No, both of you, listen to me. This is happening. Okay? This money is going through

Anne-Marie The angel. Who can never understand. <I'm so sorry, brother, sister – my stupid fault.>

Stef Anne-Marie! Just do this one thing for me. After everything I've done for you. You just tell your board it has to be spent this way. I will write down what you should say, you just read it out!

Anne-Marie has left.
   Stef wrestles the phone away from Tony and smashes it on the floor.
   Nounou and Victor have left too.
   Stef is alone. She looks around for Oudry. He is gone.

TWENTY
RESIGNATION

The band play.
    Stef is alone with her tablet.
    There is no Oudry to read her message. She reads it herself. Or uses a microphone if such a convention has been used for Oudry?

Stef Dear Huw.
    There is to be no CongoVoice festival.
    Due to a combination of NGO money, politics, diaspora relations.
    And me.
    My apols and thanks for your support both personal and professional.
    It made it all the more marked when it wasn't there. Please also consider this a resignation note.
    Yours, Stephanie Cartwright.

Elsewhere – probably as the above is taking place:
    Victor is accosted by Immigration Police. He hands them his wallet, resigned.
    They handcuff him and lead him away.
    Possibly, we see Luis.
    Free. Unbothered. Going through his tax receipts with Maurice, who is writing the details down.

TWENTY-ONE
WE ARE

Stef's flat. Stef is in old clothes. Tony stands on the threshold.

Stef That was you pressing it like a fucking panic button

Tony Your downstairs neighbour buzzed me in.

Stef Oh really, what are they like?

Tony In the last two weeks I've probably called you a hundred times. Are you alright?

Stef Yup. What are you doing here?

Tony Thought I'd come and see you on the day we were supposed to have a festival.

Stef What a horrible fucking thing to do. Come in.

Tony enters the flat.

☐

Tony You know, people actually thought you were abroad.

Stef Imaginative.

Tony What is so bad exactly? So you tried to organise a / festival

Stef Failed to / organise

Tony You tried and failed to organise a festival. Worse things happen.

Stef Yes, in the Congo. That was the point of the festival.

Tony What about next year?

Stef You're sweating.

Tony I've just had karate.

Stef *Karate* you're doing now, of course because it's 1985

Tony Because of the thing.

Stef Oh.
Yeah.
How's your karate chop?

Tony We've not covered that yet.

Stef What have you covered?

Tony If I got into a street fight right now, I would be able to bow at them and then do up my belt correctly.

Stef laughs.

Come for a walk.

Stef Where?

Tony I want to take you to see something.

He looks at a box of Stef's unpacked effects from her old office.

That's your sickbag frame. What did you do with it?

Stef I unframed it.

Tony Why?

Stef I needed to puke so I thought I'd use it for what it was meant for.

Tony Why did you need to puke?

Stef Because I drank too much guilt.

Tony What did you really do with it?

Stef Why do you care?

Tony Can I have it?

Stef You *want* my sick bag?

Tony If you haven't burned it.

Stef It's in the bin, probably at the bottom of the bin. Be my guest and dig it out.

Tony Yeah, okay.

He gets down on one knee and puts his whole arm in the bin.

□

Stef There's a better way of doing that.

Tony Probably.

He pulls the sick bag from the bin. It has sauce and coffee grits on it.
He dusts them off. He reads it to himself. He seems like he might read it out.

That's how you felt flying out of Congo?

Stef Yes.

Tony And how would you ever have found this guy, this father with the head wound?

Stef He'd be registered as an internally displaced person in a camp somewhere.

Tony And. So. Why him?

Stef I don't know. I.
I didn't look at him.

Tony folds up the bag and puts it in his pocket.

Tony I want you to come with me now.

Stef I'm not going anywhere with you, your arm's covered in shit.

Tony Put a coat on, you can come like that.

Stef Not till you tell me what for

Tony Because we booked a band and we're going to see them play.

Stef Don't be fucking weird, Tony. And insensitive.

Tony I'm serious.

Stef They're not *playing*?

Tony We booked the space, I booked the band and they're playing tonight.

Stef Why?

Tony Because we booked them.

Stef And you've not advertised.

Tony It's a closed thing.

Stef You're making this poor band perform to no public? What a waste of their time

Tony Their idea.

Stef Was it fuck

Tony They want to say they have done the gig.

Stef Can't they just lie?

Tony I don't think they want to.

■

Stef No, it's pathetic and it'll depress me even more.

Tony Gets you out the house.

Stef It's a stupid idea.

Tony So it's a stupid idea

Stef And a pointless one.

Tony And a pointless one, yes okay.

Stef The only point was to raise awareness. How much awareness will this raise?

Tony This will raise no awareness. And it's a stupid and pointless idea. But they are still playing.

Stef And no one is going.

Tony We are, Stephanie.
  We are going.
  So put your fucking coat on.

Stef ■

  She begins to put her coat on

TWENTY-TWO
LOOK AT THE WOUND

*A stage in North London. The band strike up. They are
dressed differently.*
  *They begin to perform as Rumba-stious – downbeat
Western indie song in an upbeat rumba style: 'Heaven
Knows I'm Miserable Now' by The Smiths.*
  *The band play. The music is too loud to hear anyone
speak, possibly the loudest of the show.*
  Stef and Tony are standing watching the band.
  *Anne-Marie enters. Stef and Anne-Marie look at each
other.*
  *Anne-Marie nods at her. In acknowledgement. It is not
angry. It is not affectionate.*
  *Stef gestures to Anne-Marie's eye. There is no patch.
Anne-Marie gestures she can see.*
  *Anne-Marie gestures that she's left something outside.
She returns with Suzanne.*
  They greet Suzanne. They all watch the band.
  Suzanne and Anne-Marie sway together.

A camp in South Kivu, DRC. A month later.
  *A crowd of poor Congolese men. Stef and a translator
approach them.*
  *The translator speaks to the group of men. They usher
one forward.*

It is Oudry. He is wearing a hat.
Stef speaks to Oudry through the translator, making sure to look directly at him.
The translator gestures to Oudry's head. Oudry speaks through the translator.
Stef produces some money. And pays Oudry.
Oudry lifts his hat, bows slightly and displays his wound for her to see.
Stef looks at the wound. She looks as hard and as long as she can before Oudry puts his hat back on and calmly walks away.

End of play.